The Big Yellow Book

*25 multi-purpose outlines
for pre-school groups*

Copyright © Scripture Union 2003
First published 2003, reprinted 2007, 2014

ISBN 978 1 85999 692 8

Scripture Union
207–209 Queensway
Bletchley
Milton Keynes
MK2 2EB
Email: info@scriptureunion.org.uk
Website: www.scriptureunion.org.uk

All rights reserved. The artwork and activity sheets in this publication may be photocopied for use without reference to current copyright legislation or any copyright licensing. This arrangement does not allow the printing of words or illustrations for resale or for any commercial use. Outside of this provision, no part of this publication may be reproduced, stored in a retrieval system, or transmitted in any form or by any means, electronic, mechanical, photocopying, recording or otherwise, without the prior permission of Scripture Union.

Performing Licence

If you wish to perform any of the material in this book, you are free to do so without charge, providing the performance is undertaken in an amateur context. The purchase of this book constitutes a licence granting the right to perform the pieces for no financial gain. Those wishing to engage in commercial or professional performances should make a separate approach in writing to Scripture Union.

Unless otherwise stated, Bible quotations are from the Contemporary English Version © American Bible Society, published by HarperCollins Publishers, with kind permission from the British and Foreign Bible Society.

British Library Cataloguing-in-Publication Data: a catalogue record for this book is available from the British Library.

A note on Music books

JP	*Junior Praise* (Marshall Pickering)
JU	*Jump Up If You're Wearing Red* (NS/CHP)
KS	*Kidsource* (Kevin Mayhew)
LACH	*Let's All Clap Hands!* (Scripture Union)
LSS	*Let's Sing and Shout!* (Scripture Union)

Series editors: Maggie Barfield, Sarah Mayers

Project manager: Louise Titley

Editorial support: Lizzie Green

Writers: Maggie Barfield, Susie Matheson, Kevin and Val Moore, Annette Oliver, Pam Priestley, Ruth Ranger, Priscilla Trood, Judith Wigley, Geraldine Witcher

Additional material: Mandy Catto, Rachael Champness, Sheila Clift, Marjory Francis, Alison Gidney, Mary Houlgate, Denise Niel, Margaret Spivey, Diana Turner

Cover and internal design: Mark Carpenter Design Consultants

Cover photography: Steve Shipman

Illustrations: Claire Vessey

Printed by Thomson Press India Ltd.

Acknowledgements

Thank you to Christine Orme and Christine Wood for permission to use copyright material from *Splash!*, SU 1992.

Some activities are based on material previously published in *Sing, Say and Move*, *Jigsaw*, *Let's Join In*, *Let's Praise and Pray*, *Let's Sing and Shout!* and *Let's All Clap Hands!* © Scripture Union.

Thank you to Diana Turner and Jackie Cray for so much valuable support and constructive comment.

With extra thanks to Truda Uglow from Ruth Ranger.

Scripture Union is an international Christian charity working with churches in more than 130 countries.

Thank you for purchasing this book. Any profits from this book support SU in England and Wales to bring the good news of Jesus Christ to children, young people and families and to enable them to meet God through the Bible and prayer.

Find out more about our work and how you can get involved at:
www.scriptureunion.org.uk (England and Wales)
www.suscotland.org.uk (Scotland)
www.suni.co.uk (Northern Ireland)
www.scriptureunion.org (USA)
www.su.org.au (Australia)

Contents

Introduction
by Judith Wigley

Welcome to *Tiddlywinks*...	4
Why?	6
Where and when?	7
How?	8
Playing with a purpose	9
Making the most of structure	10
Quick tips to get you started...	11
Additional resources	12
How to plan your group programme using *Tiddlywinks*	13

Easter
by Annette Oliver

1 Jesus on a donkey	Luke 19:28–38	14
2 A gift for Jesus	Mark 14:3–9	16
3 Supper time	Luke 22:7–20	20
4 Good Friday	Mark 15	22
5 Jesus is alive!	Luke 24:1–12	26
6 Easter Day	John 20:1,11–18	28
7 On the road to Emmaus	Luke 24:13–35	32
8 A barbecue on the beach	John 21:1–14	34
9 Jesus goes to heaven	Luke 24:50–53; Acts 1:9–11	38
10 Pentecost	Acts 2	40

God gives us families
by Pam Priestley, Geraldine Witcher and Maggie Barfield

11 Mothers	Genesis 18:1–15; 21:1–8	44
12 Fathers	Genesis 37:1–11	46
13 Brothers	Genesis 25:19–34; 27; 33	50
14 Sisters	Exodus 2:1–10	52
15 Families	John 4:43–54	56

Friends of Jesus
by Priscilla Trood, Maggie Barfield, Annette Oliver, Susie Matheson and Geraldine Witcher

16 Paul	Acts 9:1–19	58
17 Barnabas	Acts 4:36,37; 11:19–30	62
18 Timothy	2 Timothy 1:5–8	64
19 Lydia	Acts 16:11–15	68
20 Priscilla and Aquila	Acts 18:1–4,18–28	70

What's the weather like?
by Ruth Ranger

21 Sun	Psalm 19	74
22 Rain	1 Kings 17:1–6; 18:41–46	76
23 Wind	Acts 27	80
24 Cold	Psalm 147:15–18; Proverbs 31:13,19,21	82
25 Rainbows	Genesis 9:8–17	86

Special feature: Easter Eggstravaganza
by Kevin and Val Moore — 90

Welcome time — 92

Home time — 94

Welcome to Tiddlywinks...

Remember the game? Play it anywhere, anytime with almost any age. It can be a two-minute time filler or an afternoon of family fun captivating even the youngest child's attention. Flipping, flying coloured discs, furious scrambles after lost 'winks' and triumphant laughter as three-year-old Lucy beats Grandad again! It's so simple, such fun.

Welcome to *Tiddlywinks*... resource material for young children that's fun, flexible, and extremely user-friendly.

Fun because it's child and therefore 'play' centred. The material reflects the understanding that young children grow, develop and learn through play. *Tiddlywinks* provides young children with a wide range of enjoyable, stimulating play experiences as a basis for learning about themselves, the world in which they live and the God who made both them and that world. It's designed to be good fun!

Flexible because it is adaptable to almost any situation. The work of the Christian church is no longer restricted to Sundays as literally thousands of carers and their young children flock through the doors of our churches, halls, and community buildings between Monday and Friday. Thankfully church leaders are waking up to the fact that what happens midweek really matters, and these people are being increasingly valued as members of the extended church family. That in no way devalues the very important work that goes on during a Sunday, both within the framework of a service of worship or Sunday teaching group. BOTH Sunday and midweek work are important and of equal value, but material that's easily adaptable to a variety of different contexts needs to be flexible. *Tiddlywinks* has been written and designed with that flexibility in mind. Whether you are responsible for a midweek carer and toddler group, pram service (more likely to be called something like Butterflies, Minnows or Little Angels!), or you are a leader in a playgroup or nursery class, overseeing a Sunday crèche, teaching an early years Sunday group class, or part of a community based play centre or shoppers' crèche – there is material in *Tiddlywinks* that will be adaptable to your situation. Some of you will be looking to fill a two-hour programme, others two minutes! *Tiddlywinks*' pick-and-mix style is here to meet the needs of a wide range of contexts.

User-friendly because it is accessible to leaders who are just starting out as well as those with more experience. Whether you're wondering how to tell a Bible story, wanting to learn age-appropriate rhymes and songs, looking for creative ideas for prayer or wondering how telling the story of Noah might fit in with your early learning goals, *Tiddlywinks* can help you.

Tiddlywinks places great importance upon relationships. It recognises the crucial role of parents, carers and leaders in the development of a young child in his or her early years and the need to support and encourage all who share in this important task. Friendship between adults and children creates community, identity and a sense of belonging. When that community becomes a safe place where trust and friendship grow, both adults and children thrive within it. There could be no better foundation in the life of a young child.

OK, but you still have questions

Each outline has an activity page which can be used either in the group or at home. Photocopy as many pages as you need. Some of the craft activities recommended on these pages will work better if you photocopy them directly onto thin card instead of onto paper. Encourage adults to talk about the leaflets with the children and to do the activities together.

If the sheet is taken home, you could photocopy your group news or notices onto the blank reverse.

Where do I start…? How do I use it…? Who can use it…? Where can it be used…? When is the best time…? Why introduce spiritual topics to young children at all…? Do I need special equipment…? What skills will I need…? Will it cost anything…? Who will come…?

Everyone who has worked with young children has asked these and many other questions at some stage! The writers of *Tiddlywinks* are firmly convinced that adults learn through experience too.

In fact, 'hands-on' is the very best way to learn! No academic or paper qualification can replace first-hand experience of simply being and engaging with young children as they play and learn. The best qualifications for working with young children are a desire to be with them and a willingness to learn.

The following pages are here to help you think through questions you may have, guide your planning and preparation and help you get the best for your children from *Tiddlywinks*. We start with the all-important question WHY? If you are convinced of the reasons for working with young children, developing body, mind and spirit, you will keep going even when it feels tough. Conviction produces commitment and determination, qualities worth cultivating in any children's leader. And *Tiddlywinks* is here to help. Enjoy it!

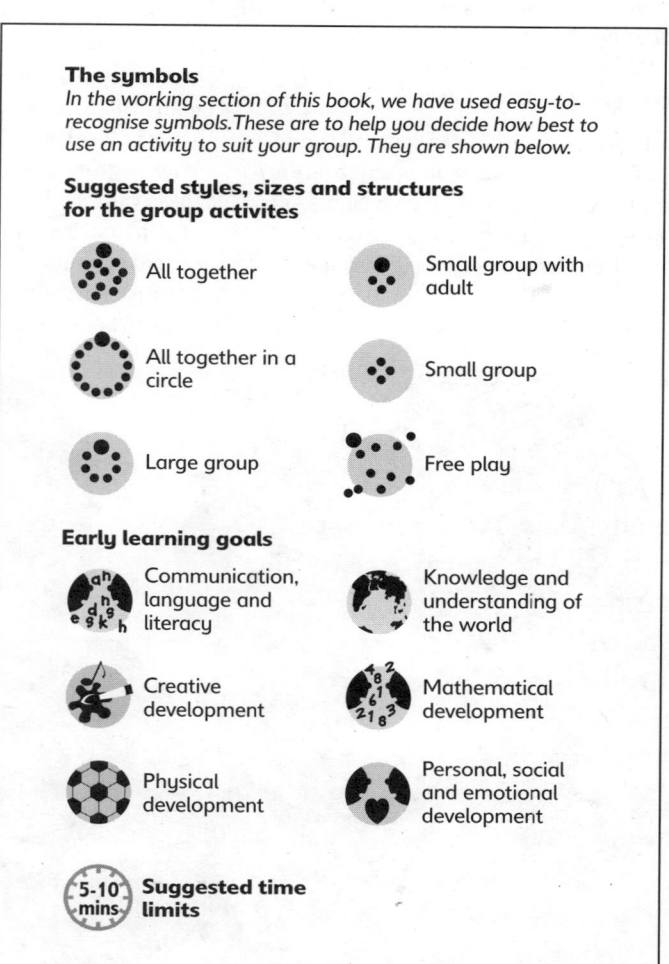

Why?

Why work with babies, toddlers and pre-schoolers? Why go to such lengths to provide appropriate play facilities, resources and materials for such young children? Let's be honest; they are noisy, messy, sometimes smelly, and thoroughly exhausting!

But, as the psalmist reminds us, they are also very special, a gift from God:

*You are the one who put me together
inside my mother's body,
and I praise you
because of the wonderful
          way you created me.*

(Psalm 139:13–14)

Few of us would deny the wonder of a new baby. The sense of miracle is often overwhelming and awe inspiring, and it isn't difficult to believe in a Creator God at such times. But the real truth behind the psalmist's words is that God's mark is upon each and every one of us right from the very beginning. From conception each one is a unique, individual human being, made in the image of God.

God's image within us is spiritual, and children (especially young children), are spiritual beings in their own right. As leaders, parents or carers of young children God gives us the awesome responsibility of sharing in his creation process. As the children in our care grow in body, mind and spirit, we become partners with God in that developmental process. Research tells us that the first five years of a child's life are the most crucial, laying down important foundations for the rest of life. If that is so, we know that we face quite a challenge. The stimulus we provide, the environment in which they grow, the quality of relationships and the values they experience will make an enormous difference to the children in our care.

Good relationships between young children and their carers are crucial for healthy growth and development. A child who experiences love, trust, security and forgiveness in their closest human relationships will quickly understand about the God who also loves, cherishes, protects and forgives them. When they become part of a community that lives out those values the impact is even greater. Their experience will make sense of all they will come to learn through the many Bible stories they hear; stories that reflect those same values and truths. When a group both practices and teaches these values it becomes a powerful place of spiritual learning for all who are part of that community. Young children and their parents and carers will thrive and grow in body, mind and spirit.

When fostered at an early age the relationship between a young child and God is transparently beautiful, often uncomplicated and spontaneous. Children are often more in touch with their spirituality than adults. They sense, they feel, they wonder but don't necessarily express those things in words. Their experience of God doesn't always need words. On several occasions in the Gospels Jesus used children as an illustration of those to whom the kingdom of God belonged encouraging adults to 'become as a child' in order to enter that kingdom (Luke 18:15–17; Mark 10:13–16; Matthew 19:13–15).

Many adults' lives have been greatly influenced by the faith of a child. By sharing in their experiences, teaching them appropriately, guiding them gently, and enabling them to grow in body, mind and spirit they too have come to a greater understanding of God, his relationship with us and plan and purpose for our lives. We live in an age where two, almost three generations of adults have had little or no positive teaching about God or experience of the church. Many of these are the parents of the children in our pre-school groups. Some of us reading these introductory pages (including the writer!) will not have received a Sunday school education but others will have been nurtured in the Christian faith from the cradle. Many of the stories we share with our children will be new to us. The action rhymes and songs of praise may be the first 'hymns' we have ever sung. Many of the ideas for prayer will be our introduction to prayer. It's a whole new journey, one in which our children will undoubtedly lead us, but a journey which, in hindsight, we shall all travel together.

Why share spiritual truths with young children? Because we all want the very best for our children and in seeking to provide the best we are all privileged to learn from them in the process.

Where and when?

Where and when you use *Tiddlywinks* material will vary considerably, as will the extent of the use of the material provided. Each session incorporates different child-centred activities linked by a theme: Play time; Game time; Making time; Story time; Rhyme time; Song time; Pray time. You may be in a position to influence everything that happens in your group and therefore, make use of any number of these. Alternatively you may have responsibility for one part of your group's programme, eg the singing time, a craft activity, or story time. The joy of *Tiddlywinks* is that you can simply extract what you need for use at any one time.

Let's look at the variety of different contexts in which pre-school groups meet and the way in which they might use *Tiddlywinks* material:

Midweek 'pram' services

Tiddlywinks contains all that a leader might need for these short, midweek 'services' of worship for pre-school children. Time may prevent them from using all the material and lack of suitable facilities may restrict the type of Play time and Making time, especially if these groups meet inside the main body of their church (although there are a number of ingenious and creative ways of adapting what might at first seem insurmountable obstacles). But, provided they have an area in which they can move safely and sit comfortably together, Game, Story, Pray, Rhyme and Song time will be ideal for these occasions.

Midweek parent/carer and toddler groups

These important groups provide a much needed meeting point in the community particularly for first time parents and carers of young children. They are led by a wide range of people, including leaders formally appointed by the church, Christian mums who attend the group with their own children, and mums, or carers, who have little contact with the church but who use (often renting) church buildings as a meeting place. Some will run along very similar lines to pram services seeking to provide a place where Christian values will be experienced and the faith taught. Others, will simply be seeking to provide quality play and creative stimulation for the children present. *Tiddlywinks* material can meet both of these needs with leaders carefully selecting what they feel is appropriate for their situation. Whilst each section is thematically linked it can also stand on its own. Linking a five-minute craft activity with a ten-minute singing time may be all that is required whilst others will incorporate a story and prayer time. It is totally flexible.

Sunday groups

Many Sunday crèches and early years teaching groups (usually for children aged two-and-a-half to five years) will be looking for a balanced teaching programme to follow over a set number of different weeks, covering the whole of the church's festivals and seasons. These children will generally come from Christian homes and families where the faith is lived as well as taught. *Tiddlywinks* will offer an extensive range of topics and themes ideally suited to this context, and of course the teaching and learning style is always child-centred and age appropriate.

Playgroups and nurseries

Most playgroups and nurseries for two-and-a-half to five-year-olds are officially registered with OFSTED and seek to follow the early years educational goals and guidelines. Leaders are trained and fully responsible for the children in their care. Whilst not written with the sole intention of meeting the educational requirements of these goals, much of the material will serve to enhance and supplement the curriculum required for these groups.

Informal settings, eg coffee mornings and drop-in centres

These informal and casual places of meeting provided by many churches regularly attract young children but rarely provide adequate facilities for them. Following five minutes of biscuit munching they are bored and restless. A simple craft activity, a couple of songs and rhymes, and a short story can make their brief visit a very valuable experience. It's a statement about how much we value these children as well as a valuable teaching opportunity. It also encourages them to return.

Special events

Many churches recognise that what happens on a Sunday morning is often inaccessible and inappropriate to young children and their families. But this does not always mean that there is not an interest in learning about and experiencing the Christian faith. Many groups are experimenting with occasional events geared entirely for young families at a time that is suitable for them. Some have found Saturday tea times a good meeting time, others Sunday afternoons. Festivals, ie Christmas, Easter, Harvest etc are excellent starting points for these and often draw large numbers of people, especially when food is part of the programme. The *Tiddlywinks* special feature (designed for big group events – see pages 90 and 91) and/or *Tiddlywinks* session material can be creatively used to provide a theme base with all the necessary ingredients for an enjoyable family-friendly programme.

How?

How?

When setting out to run a group for pre-school children and their carers there are practical things to consider which are essential, others that are recommended and others still that are a bonus. This page outlines all three. It also includes a recommended plan of action for any who might be starting from scratch.

ESSENTIAL

Health and safety

Imagine the building to be used for the group as your own home and apply the same levels of health and safety requirements. Check heaters, floor surfaces, furniture, plug sockets, secure entry and exit points, fire exits, toilet and baby changing facilities, kitchen hygiene and safety if serving refreshments. Be aware of the different allergies that could affect children and encourage leaders to attend a First Aid course. Aim for the highest possible standards of health and safety at all times.

Child Protection

In the UK, the 1989 Children's Act is designed to encourage good practice and safety in all work undertaken with children aged 0–18 years of age, including that in churches. Any church-sponsored group where children remain in the care of leaders for longer than two hours, and which meets more than six times a year, is required to register with the Social Services department of the local authority. Many of our playgroups and nurseries fall into this category, but parent/carer and toddler groups do not need to register, although many choose to notify local authorities of their existence. Where parents and carers remain with their children for the duration of the session they are held responsible for their own children. Each church denomination or network has drawn up its own guidelines for good practice with recommendations for group leaders working in this context. These can be obtained from national headquarters or through regional children's advisers and should be followed carefully in order to maintain the highest of standards possible.

If you are working outside the UK, please check up on the Child Protection legislation for your area.

Insurance cover

Insurance for pre-school groups should have appropriate and adequate cover. Existing church policies should always be checked. Specialist agencies such as the *Pre-School Learning Alliance* or *Playgroup Network* work with major insurance companies to provide tailor-made packages for pre-school groups.

RECOMMENDED

Storage facilities

You can never have enough storage! What might start as one plastic box full of toys and materials will quickly multiply. Borrow, beg, plead and cry for more boxes, shelves, cupboards and storerooms that are easily accessible; make setting out and clearing away as easy as possible

Keeping records

The fire service require a written record of all persons in a public building at any time which provides a very useful record of all who have attended. Additional information such as addresses, phone numbers, birth dates help to inform members in the event of unexpected group closure due to bad weather or sickness, and to acknowledge birthdays of children, all of which shows care and concern. Ensure, however, that confidentiality is maintained with all personal details kept on file. In accordance with the Data Protection Act, do not divulge any information to third parties.

A photocopiable registration form can be found on the inside front cover of *Tiddlywinks: The Big Red Book*.

Teamwork

This work requires storytellers, singers, craft specialists, people who will keep a register, take monies, make refreshments, set out and clear away, etc. Where teamwork is fostered it also becomes a training ground for future leaders: those making coffee may develop into wonderful storytellers, songwriters or craft workers. Try to create an atmosphere where people are free to learn and you will grow your own leaders naturally.

Budgeting

Much of this work incorporates both the spiritual nurture of children and outreach to carers and families. Many churches allocate a specific amount of budget money for this purpose but don't always recognise the context in which it is being done. Be sure to remind them and ask for ongoing financial support to fund the work. Training leaders, publicity, resource books, craft materials, play equipment, refreshments and various other miscellaneous items can be costly. Keep a record of expenditure and income, with proof of purchases at all times. Don't be worried about making a charge for the group, as many parents/carers are more than willing to contribute towards something that their children enjoy.

BONUS

Behind the scene helpers

There are many housebound people in our churches who love to be involved in children's work. Publicity, programmes and newsletters can be designed on computers; craft materials cut and prepared well in advance and prayer can be a vital and encouraging support to a tired and weary leader. A little advance planning can alleviate a lot of pressure when shared with willing home-based workers.

Outside funding

Occasionally groups have benefited from charitable grants. Different bodies vary considerably in the criteria set out for funding – many decline groups that promote religious activities whilst others seem much more open. Local libraries usually have details of local and national charities.

If starting your group from scratch you should always seek the permission and support of your church leadership body. Go equipped with a well thought through plan of action.

Playing with a purpose

Play is the basis for almost every part of the *Tiddlywinks* material because the writers know and understand that young children learn everything through playing. Their capacity to listen is limited to just one minute for each year of life and so the suggestions offered include very few 'listening only' activities. In recent years educationalists have confirmed that all ages of children and adults learn far more through what they do and experience than simply through what they hear.

Each part of the theme-based *Tiddlywinks* programme is designed to offer young children some kind of play with a purpose. As a child moves from one activity to another, joining in small and large group experiences, he or she is gathering understanding and experience of that topic or theme. Of course some won't make the connections, but others will.

What is most important is that each activity is accessible and meaningful and it is the leader's task to provide the basic ingredients and stimulus for creating the best possible, purposeful play experience. Let's consider the different play sections of the programme:

Play time

(unstructured play)
'Play time' describes a variety of unstructured play activities, many of which will connect with children's every day life and experiences. This is likely to take up the bulk of the session and greet children on arrival. It will help introduce them to the day's topic, eg animals for story of Noah, boats for story of Jesus and the storm, food for story of feeding 5,000 etc, acquire the vocabulary (when stimulated by adults) for use in the songs and rhymes, and explore concepts, eg animal families, effects of water, sharing out food between friends and dolls. All these play experiences are valuable in their own right but also become important foundations in a programme designed to help young children learn about a specific Christian story or Bible truth.

Game time

(cooperative play)
Young children generally play alone but simple, non-competitive games will develop an awareness of others and a sense of belonging to a group. They will learn to share, take turns, watch (and imitate) others, express delight in both their own and others' achievements, and respond to each other. Physically active games also stimulate physical development especially coordination and balance. Games can strengthen relationships within a group and help create a community built on Christian values, as well as provide a greater understanding and experience of the story or theme being developed.

Story time

(engaging play)
When creatively led, a story time demands much more than just listening. Most Bible stories lend themselves to visual, sound and action aids, actively engaging as many of the children's senses as you possibly can. Participation will involve ears, voices, hands (and legs) but also the emotions. Young children will live through the characters they are introduced to, imagining, feeling, sensing, and exploring all aspects of the story you are telling. They may not be able to respond with words but they will be learning.

Making time

(creative play)
Creative play introduces young children to a whole new world. The learning here most definitely takes place in the process of making and not in the end product, even though it will be greatly cherished and a very important reminder of the day's theme or story. Size, shape, texture, colour and patterns are just some of the important discoveries that will be made through making. Children will explore a variety of materials and acquire new skills and techniques. Together parents, carers and children will grow in confidence and creativity; they will uncover the mark of a creative God within them, in whose image they have been made. Whatever the limitations on your space and facilities make 'Making time' possible, as it is one of the most valuable learning experiences of all.

Song time and Rhyme time

(musical play)
Music, rhythm, rhyme and movement are experiences of the womb so it's not surprising that even the youngest of babies will actively respond to this part of the programme. When part of a circle time the learning is far more than simply the words of songs and rhymes being used. Young children learn to listen, follow actions, take turns, recognise each other and be part of a group experience. Even those who appear not to be participating amaze parents by repeating everything they have learnt hours later when at home!

Adults too

Never underestimate all that adults are learning through the children's play programme. Some are actually learning how to play themselves; others are learning Bible stories and truths for the first time; and others will want to develop that learning through further adult-centred programmes. *Tiddlywinks* even provides suggestions for ways in which you might help them to do so.

Making the most of structure

Under-fives love routine and structure. They learn through rhythm and repetition. It makes them feel secure and safe and helps them to quickly identify people, situations and experiences. As these become positive experiences children will look for them, ask for them and sometimes be very difficult to handle when they don't get them!

Structure doesn't mean boring repetition or inflexibility. It is determined by the basic needs of the children in our care. Every child needs to eat (even if they don't want to!) and so the structure of our day includes several eating times, but, exactly when, where and what we eat is determined by the individual's needs and circumstances. In the same way, a group including young children and their carers needs to have a structure that has been fashioned and shaped to meet the needs and circumstances of its members.

Tiddlywinks material is shaped into a structure that incorporates several important components; 'welcome' time; 'circle' time and 'home' time. Each are created to produce familiarity and security for both carers and children.

Welcome time
Providing a welcome is all about creating a sense of belonging, being part of a community. The key to doing it lies in being ready. Try out the ideas on pages 92 and 93.

Ready for children
The room or area being used should act like a magnet to every child so that they are immediately drawn into a play activity of some kind. Pre-schoolers are not able to sit around waiting for everyone to arrive! They need to play. When setting out your room make safe provision for babies and early toddlers, keep large pieces of equipment and mobile toys away from activity tables and encourage adult participation by positioning chairs close to activity tables.

Ready for adults
Establishing eye contact and welcoming individuals by name are the two most important acts of welcome. A one-to-one personal approach helps adults feel they and their children belong to a caring community. It reflects the love and care that Christians know God has for each individual.

Ready for newcomers
Newcomers need special treatment. First experiences are lasting ones and once put off they rarely give you a second chance. A leader should be allocated specifically to the task of welcoming new adults and children. Often there are details that need to be taken and procedures to explain which take time. It can also be helpful to provide a little leaflet describing the group, its purpose and structure, giving useful contact numbers.

Tiddlywinks provides a number of suggestions for activities that help build a sense of welcome. Remember whatever you choose, it will necessitate you being ready – the most important welcome factor of them all!

Circle time
Circle time is all about communication, for which you will need to be prepared. It's about preparing any number of the story, rhyme, song and prayer activities suggested in the *Tiddlywinks* material to engage both children and adults within a simple circle. The 'circle' shape is important as it includes everyone and brings them into a position where they can see and join in with what is happening. Participation by everyone is crucial to the success of circle time and many groups choose to go into a separate area or room to avoid distractions of toys and equipment; others simply clear away before starting. This time is key to developing the sense of belonging and group ownership from which will grow shared responsibility and strong community ties.

When you are part of a community you share special occasions together. It may be a birthday (adult's or child's!), special anniversary (of the group or church) or celebration of a newborn baby. Circle time is the ideal time to focus on these special occasions. There may also be sad times for which the group as a whole need to find an expression of shock, grief or sorrow, eg bereavement of a child, a national tragedy, a local concern. The simple lighting of a candle, a song or prayer may be sensitively incorporated into this special time together.

Home time
So far, creating our structure has involved being ready and being prepared. Ensuring a positive home time means we have to be organised. Too often under-fives groups simply disintegrate with no positive means of finishing or saying goodbye. People drift away as leaders scurry around tidying up. A positive ending gives a feeling of satisfaction and completion and develops a sense of anticipation for the next meeting.

Many group sessions end with a circle time building in a final song or rhyme that indicates 'this is the end'. *Tiddlywinks* offers a number of different ways in which you can mark the end in this way. Look at the ideas on page 94 and try to choose one that best suits your group, and let it become part of your routine.

Quick tips to get you started...

Many experienced children's leaders find working with groups of young children daunting, especially when parents and carers are present. The skills and confidence required are quite different to those needed to work with older children. If you are new to this age range, or it has been some years since you've had contact with them, spend some time simply being with them and familiarising yourself with their behaviour and play patterns. You will be amazed at how quickly you acquire the knowledge and experience necessary for leading various parts of the *Tiddlywinks* programme. Here are a few tips to get you started:

● Using the Bible with young children

Do explain that the Bible is God's very special storybook

Do show the children a child-friendly Bible each time you tell a Bible story so that they become familiar with it

Do make it accessible to them and encourage them to borrow a copy to take home

Don't read straight from the Bible, always 'tell' a story

Do communicate an enthusiasm and excitement for the stories you tell, remembering that you share God's story

Do be prepared for the many questions that some children will ask!

● Storytelling

Do make it short (remember one minute of attention for each year of a child's life)

Do sit where you can see and be seen

Do make it visual, eg large pictures, household objects, puppets, Duplo, or toys

Do involve the children in actions, sounds, and repetitive phrases

Do give them time and space to respond to the stories with their comments and questions

Don't be worried about repeating the story, especially if they have enjoyed it!

● Leading songs and rhymes

Don't worry about not being able to play an instrument

Do sit at the children's level when leading

Don't teach more than one new song at any one time

Don't pitch songs and rhymes too high or use complex tunes

Do use children's instruments but,

Don't forget to put them away afterwards

Do encourage parents and carers to join in

Do use familiar tunes and write your own words

● Behaviour

Do make sure that parents and carers know they are responsible for their children

Do offer support to a parent/carer whose child is going through a difficult stage

Don't discuss the behaviour of their child in front of others

Do remember there is nearly always a reason for bad behaviour, eg boredom, neglect, inappropriate play, tiredness, hunger etc

Do develop positive strategies for dealing with common behaviour patterns in young children, eg biting, pushing, unwillingness to share, tantrums, dirty nappy!

Do encourage parents and carers to deal with difficult behaviour and

Don't intervene unless a child is in danger

● Craft

Do protect tables, floors and children if using messy materials

Do supervise at all times

Do let the children do the activity! (Provide additional materials if adults want a go.)

Don't worry too much about the end product

Do have hand-washing facilities ready

Don't allow the activity to go on too long

Do create drying space for activities needing to dry

Do be sure to put the child's name on the activity at the start

Do allow children to take them home – make more if you need a display

Do make the most of creating displays – it is a presence of the group in their absence

● Prayer

Do make prayers short, simple and spontaneous

Do try using a candle, bell or simple prayer song to introduce a prayer time

Do encourage different kinds of prayer, eg 'thank you', 'sorry' and 'please' prayers

Don't always insist on hands together, eyes closed

Do encourage action, rhyme and song prayers

Don't miss the opportunity to send written prayers into the home through craft activities

Do consider writing your own special prayer for the group that the children can learn and grow familiar with

● Involving parents and carers

Do spend time fostering good friendships with parents and carers

Do make clear to them that they are responsible for their children

Do encourage maximum participation at all times

Don't expect a parent/carer with more than one child to carry responsibility for activities

Do look out for hidden talents and leadership skills

Don't reject genuine offers of help and support

Do affirm, support and encourage parents and carers at all times.

Working with young children is hard work but we gain far more than we ever give. Be warned – shopping in your local supermarket will never be the same again. You will be gurgled at, sung to, waved at and clearly shouted at from one end of the freezers to the other. Entering the world of young children in your community will provide you with a whole new family! And together you will become part of God's family.

Additional resources

to help and support you in your work with young children and their parents/carers.

Recommended children's Bibles and storybooks

The Beginner's Bible (Zondervan)

The Lion First Bible (Lion Publishing)

Lift the Flap Bible (Candle Books)

Me Too! Books, Marilyn Lashbrook (Candle Books) 16 different titles with interactive stories from both the New and Old Testament

Tiddlywinks: My Little Red Book – First Steps in Bible Reading, Ro Willoughby; *My Little Blue Book*, Penny Boshoff; *My Little Yellow Book*, Leena Lane and Penny Boshoff; *My Little Green Book*, Christine Wright (Scripture Union)

Action Rhyme series, Stephanie Jeffs (Scripture Union) 4 titles:
Come into the Ark with Noah; March Round the Walls with Joshua; Follow the Star with the Wise Men; Share out the Food with Jesus

Bible Concertina books, Nicola Edwards and Kate Davies (Scripture Union)
The Creation; Noah's Ark; The Christmas Baby

The Bible Pebbles series, Tim and Jenny Wood (Scripture Union) *Daniel in the Lion's Den; Jonah and the Big Fish; Moses in the Basket; Noah's Ark; The First Christmas; The First Easter; Jesus the Healer; Jesus the Teacher*

The Little Fish series, Gordon Stowell (Scripture Union) Lots of titles about Jesus, other Bible people, and you and me

Jigsaw Bible Activity Books 2, 3 and 4 (Scripture Union)

Things Jesus Did, Stories Jesus Told, People Jesus Met, Baby Jesus, Stephanie Jeffs (Bible Reading Fellowship)

Prayer books

Pray and Play: 101 Creative Prayer Ideas for Use with Under-fives, Kathy L Cannon (Scripture Union)

The Pick a Prayer Series, Tim and Jenny Wood, illustrated by Suzy-Jane Tanner (Scripture Union), 4 spiral-bound board titles:
Pick-a-prayer: For Bedtime; Pick-a-prayer: For Every Day; Pick-a-prayer: For Special Days; Pick-a-prayer: To Say Thank You

My Little Prayer Box, (Scripture Union)

Hello God, it's Me, Stephanie King and Helen Mahood (Scripture Union)

The Lion Book of First Prayers, Sue Box (Lion Publishing)

What Shall We Pray About? Andy Robb (Candle)

Prayers with the Bears, (John Hunt Publishing) 4 titles

101 Ideas for Creative Prayer, New Ideas for Creative Prayer, Judith Merrell (Scripture Union)

Song/rhyme books

Let's Sing and Shout! ed. Maggie Barfield (Scripture Union)

Let's All Clap Hands! ed. Maggie Barfield (Scripture Union)

Jump Up If You're Wearing Red (NS/CHP)

Feeling Good!, Peter Churchill (NS/CHP)

Bobby Shaftoe, Clap your Hands, Sue Nicholls, (A&C Black) includes 37 familiar and traditional tunes with simple guitar chords.

Kidsource Books 1 and 2 (Kevin Mayhew). A general selection for children, including many suitable for under-fives.

Other resources

God and Me series, exploring emotions and Christian beliefs (Scripture Union):
Really, Really Scared; Really, Really Excited; I Love You; I Miss You, Leena Lane
What's Heaven Like?; What's God Like?; What's in the Bible?; Can Jesus Hear Me? Stephanie King

Resources to support parents and carers

Lion Pocketbook Series, various authors (Lion Publishing). Over 15 different titles on both faith-searching issues, eg *Why Believe?; Why Pray?*, and pastoral issues, eg *Why Marry?; When a child dies*. These are inexpensive pocketbooks ideal for use with parents and carers.

First Steps, video for parents inquiring about infant baptism, (CPAS)

Welcome to Baptism, Journey of a Lifetime Video, Grayswood Studio

Time out for Parents, Positive Parenting Publications, First Floor, 2A South Street, Gosport PO12 1ES. A comprehensive teaching pack, covering most aspects of parenting from infancy to teenage years

Just a Minute: Biblical Reflections for Busy Mums, Christine Orme (Scripture Union)

Family Caring Trust
Director: Michael Quinn, 44 Rathfriland Rd, Newry, Co. Down, N Ireland BT34 1LD
The Family Caring Trust produce an extensive range of parenting courses focusing on different age ranges of children. These have been widely used and appreciated in pre-school community groups.

CARE for the Family PO Box 448
Cardiff CF15 7YY
CARE produce a wide range of resources to support parents including a video based course called Parent Talk, books, training and special parent and child weekends.

Courses for parents/carers who wish to explore questions and issues of faith:

Emmaus, National Society

Alpha, Holy Trinity Brompton

Additional leaders' resource material

SALT 3 to 4+ for leaders and *Sparklers* activity material for children (Scripture Union)

Tiddlywinks: The Big Red, Blue, Yellow and Green Books/My Little Red, Blue, Yellow and Green Books (Scripture Union)

Glitter and Glue: 101 Creative Craft Ideas for Use with Under-fives, Annette Oliver (Scripture Union)

Praise Play and Paint, Jan Godfrey (NS/CHP)

Under Fives Alive and *Under Fives – Alive and Kicking*, Farley, Goddard, Jarvis, (NS/CHP)

Bible Fun for the Very Young, Vicki Howe (Bible Reading Fellowship)

Bible Stuff, Janet Gaukroger (CPAS) 5 titles in the series.

The following 2 titles are packed with ideas for encouraging parents and children to celebrate the Christian year at home:
Feast of Faith, Kevin and Stephanie Parkes (NS/CHP)
The 'E' Book, Gill Ambrose (NS/CHP)

Background reading

Working with Under 6s, Val Mullally (Scripture Union)

Children Finding Faith, Francis Bridger (Scripture Union/CPAS)

Bringing Children to Faith, Penny Frank (Scripture Union/CPAS)

Children and the Gospel, Ron Buckland (Scripture Union)

The Adventure Begins, Terry Clutterham (Scripture Union/CPAS)

Seen and Heard, Jackie Cray (Monarch)

Sharing Jesus with Under Fives, Janet Gaukroger (Crossway Books)

Networks and organisations supporting work with young children

Pre-school Learning Alliance
61-63 Kings Cross Rd, London WC1X 9LL

Playgroup Network, PO Box 23, Whitely Bay, Tyne and Wear, NE26 3DB

Scripture Union
207-209 Queensway, Bletchley, Milton Keynes, MK2 2EB. www.scriptureunion.org.uk
For readers in other countries, please contact your national Scripture Union office for details.

The Mothers' Union
24 Tufton St, London SW1P 3RB

Church Pastoral Aid Society
Jackie Cray, Adviser for Families and Under-fives, Athena Drive, Tachbrook Park, Warwick CV34 6NG

How to plan your group programme using Tiddlywinks

Tiddlywinks Big Books provide resources, ideas and activities for use in any pre-school setting. Whether you are running a carer-and-toddler group; a playgroup or pre-school; a nursery or nursery school; a child-minding network; a crèche or toddler club; a conventional Sunday morning group at church; a drop-in centre, a coffee morning or a pram service – or any other place or group where under-fives gather together – *Tiddlywinks* has suggestions to help you.

Here, some pre-school practitioners choose their own options for their own different types of group, using the topic 'Barnabas' on pages 62, 63, 66.

Some of our volunteers didn't like the original song in this outline – so we've written a new one!

Anita's choice

Play time: children under three love to explore tactilely and would enjoy simple puzzles and shape sorters. We'd encourage drawing, colouring and sorting and adapt the dressing up and shop play, making it simpler for younger children. We do a lot of playing! I would use the prayer but wouldn't expect the children to repeat line-by-line. And I'd simplify the game so we could use it with younger children.

Anita leads a church crèche for under-threes, with about five children coming each time. She says, 'Overall this is good material, most suitable I think for 3 to 5s but I could adapt some ideas for my 0 to 3s.'

Sue's choice

Children need activities to arrive to: I would select from the play ideas, encouraging them to play together and helping tidy up too. I would make the banner using the cutting and sticking method; and the story, using a cut-out of Barnabas from the activity page as a visual aid. I would read the prayer but point out first how the children have been sharing and caring during the morning. Time limits mean I'd prefer to use the prayer idea to the game. Children like to have a take-home sheet, but we might use the activity page in the session instead. The idea for adults would not apply in our group.

Sue has been a helper in a Sunday morning church group for nearly twenty years. The group meets for 50 minutes during the church service and joins with the whole congregation towards the end.

Denise teaches a nursery class of 54 children, attached to a First School. Ten percent of the 3 to 4-year-old children have special needs.

Denise's choice

Play time is great stuff, encompassing the true learning through play ethos. This is particularly good for a larger group. I would use the prayer but preface it with a discussion about positive behaviour.

Other activities would not be done with the whole group. Game, making and story would work with smaller groups. The story is good and interactive; but the rhyme is a bit 'twee'. I'd use the other activities to encourage good behaviour and kindness. I would use the idea from the activity page to make a large scale display to encourage all the children to be actively involved.

Kathy helps coordinate a group of 20 or more under-fives and their carers. She also leads a pram service. Both are church-based and the church sees ministry with under-fives as one of the vital areas of church life.

Kathy's choices

For children-and-carers group

Play time, because play is vitally important for development. For informal worship, I'd choose the story, rhyme, song and prayer. Leaders aim to talk to every child and adult each week so 'adults too' reflects what we do. I'd have some copies of the activity page and crayons available on a table with one or two adults there to supervise as an activity for those over about two and a half.

For pram service

Story time is the focal point of the service, with children sitting on a carpet where they can see pictures and visual aids. We like to introduce new rhymes and songs, along with familiar ones. Prayer is something we emphasise. We'd make it a time to pray quietly for those we know who are ill or need help. We make time for play and I'd use the activity page, though sadly adults don't always value children's scribbles and leave their efforts behind.

Martin's choice

'We'd make a large banner with every child adding a bit more during the day. A great decoration for the room afterwards. While the children are working, I'll be telling the story – just to one or two children at a time. By the end of the morning, I might have told the same story twenty times!'

Martin helps at a shoppers' drop-in on church premises. He says, 'There's no time for a programme or anything very structured. Children might stay for an hour or only as long as it takes their mum to down a cup of coffee!'

1 Easter
Jesus on a donkey

Luke 19: 28–38

Play time

Ride a donkey
You will need: a rocking horse, hobby-horses (make your own by stuffing a sock with kapok, adding features including long ears, and lashing this to a broom handle (or similar) to make a hobby-donkey), horse-on-wheels toys.

Make sure all the children who want to, get a ride. Use appropriate language (walk, trot, bridle, etc) to help the children get involved in the activity.

Provide some plush toy donkeys for younger children to cuddle.

Donkey makers
Prepare some donkey puzzles by drawing or copying a donkey picture onto card and cutting into several jigsaw pieces. You could enlarge and copy the donkey on Activity page 18 which goes with this session. Make several puzzles with 2–8 pieces for children to try out. (Keep the puzzles separate by using different colour card for each one.)

Carnival time
Provide lots of unusual fabrics, hats, masks and wings as well as your usual dressing-up clothes and encourage children to create their own carnival costumes. Show some pictures of the costumes used in carnivals at Rio de Janeiro or Notting Hill, or even local events. Play some Latin American dance music and have your own procession around the room. Those who have not dressed up can join in by forming a crowd, clapping, waving and cheering.

Be a donkey
Pretend to be donkeys carrying heavy loads on your backs. If you have a suitable area, let children go on all fours and pretend to be donkeys. Put light loads on their backs – a teddy or a blanket for a saddle. (Don't let children ride on each other, for safety reasons.)

For an informal craft activity, enlarge the donkey shape on the Activity page to full size (you could project it on to a huge piece of card) and collage on pieces of screwed up grey tissue or crêpe paper.

Game time

Tail on the donkey
To play this game you need a large outline of a donkey, without a tail. Cut out a tail and place a blob of Blu tack on one end. Cover the child's eyes with a loosely tied scarf or ask them to close their eyes very tightly. Give them the tail and steer them towards the picture: let them choose where to stick the tail on. Write their name on the spot where they pinned the tail. Repeat for each child. (With very young children play this game in small groups, as they do not have a long attention span.) Keep the game exciting and fast moving. It doesn't matter who has got the closest tail: they will enjoy playing in a non-competitive way.

Making time

Donkey ears
You will need: strips of card 6 cm deep and long enough to go round a child's head, grey card, sticky tape, scissors, crayons.

Cut two long donkey ears from grey card.

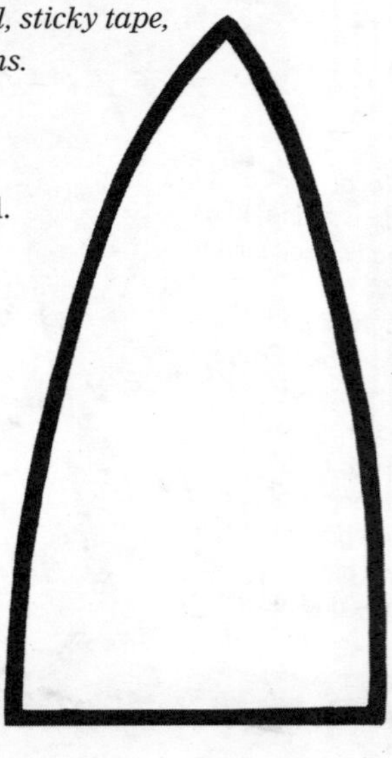

Allow the child to decorate the band and ears with the crayons. When they have finished, place the band around their head to find the right size, and secure with tape. Cut off any excess card. Tape the ears to the inside of the band, lining up roughly with the child's own ears.

Flags
Make simple flags by tying or taping pieces of lightweight strong paper or fabric to 20 cm lengths of smooth garden cane. Enjoy waving the flags in the air or save them for a play-procession, during another part of your session.

Story time

Jesus on a donkey
As you tell this story, invite the children (and adults!) to come with you to join the crowd following Jesus.

It's morning. The sun shines brightly as Jesus and his friends walk along the road. They are going towards a big city, called Jerusalem. Sometimes they sing as they walk along. Now other people come and join them. Children skip along with their mums and dads. They are all going towards the big city. Let's go with them…

Jesus is quiet as he walks along. He's going to the big city too. He calls to two of his friends, 'Go ahead,' he says, 'you'll find a young donkey which has never given anyone a ride before. Please bring him to me.'

Jesus stops and waits. All the people stop too. Let's stop with them… What is going to happen? Listen! They whisper to each other, 'Is Jesus going to show us that he's our king?'

Listen! What's that sound? It's the clip-clop clip-clop of donkey's hooves on the road. Here come Jesus' two friends and they've brought the donkey with them. They lead the donkey to Jesus. They take off their coats and put them on the donkey's back. They help Jesus get on. Off they go again, with Jesus riding on the donkey. Come on, let's go…

Now what's happening? Look! The people in the crowd are taking off their coats too! They are laying them down on the dusty road, all the way along the road to the big city. Listen! They are shouting, 'Jesus is our king! He's coming to our city. Now everything will be good for us again.'

Jesus tells the donkey to walk on. The people in the crowd cheer and wave. They watch as Jesus rides the donkey along the road and over the people's coats! Everyone cheers again! 'Hooray for Jesus! Hooray! Here comes our king, riding on a donkey!'

All the way into the big city the people cheer and wave. Let's shout and wave too…

Jesus is still quiet. He looks ahead, towards the big city. It's a happy day but Jesus knows that soon he will have to do something very hard; something that God wants him to do. We'll hear more about that another time, but just for now, let's follow the crowd and shout with them: 'Jesus is our king! Hooray for Jesus!'

Rhyme time

Riding on a donkey
Liven up this rhyme with shouting and acting out being part of the crowd welcoming Jesus.

Sing a song and shout for joy,
Happy is each girl and boy.
Shout for King Jesus!
He's off to Jerusalem.
He's off to Jerusalem,
He's off to Jerusalem,
Riding on a donkey,
He's off to Jerusalem.

It was early in the day
Jesus started on his way.
Wave and shout for Jesus!
He's off to Jerusalem.
He's off to…

Shout for Jesus everyone,
For we know he is God's son.
Shout for King Jesus,
He's off to Jerusalem.
He's off to…

Song time

Jesus went to Jerusalem
Choose a child to be Jesus and ride a hobby-donkey round the room while everyone else pretends to be the crowd. Sing to the tune of 'The mulberry bush' as you wave streamers or flags. Repeat as many times as you wish, with other children taking the role of Jesus.

Jesus went to Jerusalem,
  Jerusalem, Jerusalem,
Jesus went to Jerusalem,
  riding on a donkey.

The people they all waved and cheered,
  waved and cheered, waved and cheered,
The people they all waved and cheered,
  at Jesus on a donkey.

Jesus showed that he's a king,
  he's a king, he's a king,
Jesus showed that he's a king
  by riding on a donkey.

Jesus Christ is our king too,
  our king too, our king too,
Jesus Christ is our king too.
  We can love and praise him.

Pray time

My God is very great!
Praise chant from Psalm 104.

My *(Thumbs pointing to self.)*
God *(Thumbs pointing upwards.)*
Is very great!
He gives water for donkeys to drink. *(Hands to side of head to make ears.)*

My God is very great!
He gives bread to make me strong. *(Flex arm muscles.)*

My God is very great!
He plants trees for the birds to nest in. *(Stretch arms wide.)*

All these things my God has done. *(Circle arms.)*
Thank you God! You are very great!

Let the children draw something God has done which they think is great. (You could give them a donkey-shaped piece of paper to draw on.) Repeat the chant and this time, hold up the drawings, instead of doing actions.

Extra time

•Sing all your favourite lively praise songs and celebrate like the people in the crowd who were so excited to see Jesus. Learn these words, to 'Ring-o-roses': 'We can sing for Jesus, we can sing for Jesus, here comes Jesus, we all praise the king!'

•Play 'Hunt the donkey', hiding a model or soft toy donkey somewhere in the room for the children to find.

Adults too

What sort of child-friendly Easter events are planned for your church or in your local area? Maybe even a Palm Sunday procession? Think about how to advertise these and how best to invite those who attend your group and their families. How about running an Easter Eggstravaganza? (see pages 90–91) This is an event for all ages, but with particular bias towards the youngest children.

Jesus went from 'hero' to 'zero'. Within less than a week, people who showed their joy and expectation by throwing their coats along the road, were shouting for Jesus' death. We know this is what life is like: the football crowd adores the goalkeeper who stops the ball – but if he fails, everyone quickly turns against him. Maybe some of the adults feel that way about their relationship with God. They may feel let down, deserted, as if God has not met their expectations and needs. Can you provide a safe environment where they can share their doubts and be listened to?

Top tip

Usborne Bible Tales: *The Easter Story* by Heather Amery. This great book tells the Easter story in simple text at the top of the page, and in more detail at the bottom of the page. It is ideal as your child grows and develops. *RSVP* by Peter Grant, SU, is an ideal introduction for adults to what the Bible has to say about Jesus.

ACTIVITY PAGE:
The photocopiable activity page for this outline is on page 18

2 Easter
A gift for Jesus

Mark 14: 3–9

Play time

Fresh air
Just before people arrive, spray your meeting area liberally with perfumed air freshener: see if anyone comments on the smell! Choose a strong perfume or aftershave to wear yourself: dab some on the back of your hand and let the children smell it.

Guess the smell
Prepare a display of different smells. Rub or spray separate pieces of card with things like perfume, wax polish, baby bath liquid, toothpaste. Leave these to dry and they will still retain an aroma. Put other distinctive items, like herbs or coffee, into pots with a gauze lid so that children can smell them but not inhale. Individual items like oranges, new bars of soap and a freshly baked bread roll can be set out too. An adult needs to stay by the display during your free play session, so that children can explore the smells safely. The adult can also stimulate discussion about the different scents.

Gifts!
Cover some boxes and lids (shoe boxes are ideal for this) with colourful wrapping paper. Let the children choose items from your toy collection to put in the boxes and give as pretend presents to each other, to their parents and carers or even to the dolls and cuddly toys. Have fun trying to guess what is in the box and then seeing if you are right. Do remember to stress that this is a pretend game and that the presents are not to take home!

Game time

Pairs
Make up some cards using the faces shown. Label with the character's name. Lay all the cards face down on a table. Encourage two children to play together. A child turns over two cards at a time, trying to find a matching pair. If they find a pair, the cards are put to one side; if not, both are turned face down again and play passes to the other child.

Jesus   Simon

woman

Guess the parcel
You will need: several recognisable (unbreakable!) everyday items such as a large spoon, cushion, teddy, bucket, tennis racquet.

Wrap each item in wrapping paper, making sure the shape is still recognisable. Put the items into a box so that they cannot be seen by the children. Settle the children in a circle. Take one item from the box at a time and pass it around the circle. When it comes back to you ask if anyone knows what it is. Give the item to a child to unwrap and see if you were right!

Making time

Perfumed pictures
You will need: thick card, PVA glue and spreaders, dried flower pot pourri, ribbon.

Give each child a simple shape cut from the card. Let them coat one side in glue and then press on pieces of pot pourri. Glue a loop of ribbon to the back so the picture can hang up and perfume the air around it. (Make sure children wash their hands thoroughly after this activity and do not try eating the pot pourri: some of the coloured pieces can look very attractive.) This makes a perfumed gift for the child to take home.

Smell the flowers
You will need: art materials, perfume, cotton wool balls.

Let children make a picture of flowers by painting, drawing or collage. When the picture is complete and dry, put some flowery perfume onto a piece of cotton wool and let the child rub it over the picture to add a flowery smell. (You can use a flower-scented air freshener or polish instead, but always use cotton wool to transfer it onto the picture.)

Story time

A special gift
Begin the story by 'finding' an empty perfume bottle. Say, 'What's this? A perfume bottle! It looks pretty. I'm sure the perfume smelled pretty too. There's someone with a bottle of perfume in our story about Jesus. Listen to who it is and what she did with the bottle…'

Then tell the story as follows.

Jesus could do all sorts of wonderful things. He could make people who were ill better. One of the people he made better was a man called Simon. Now Simon was well again, he asked Jesus and his friends to a meal at his house. They all sat down and started eating their food. While they were eating, they saw that a woman had walked into the house. She was carrying something in her hands. She was being very careful. What could it be?

The woman was carrying a bottle of perfume.

Before anyone could ask her who she was or why she had come, the woman went to Jesus. She took the lid off the bottle, and she poured the perfume onto Jesus' head! What a strange thing to do! All the perfume ran into his hair, and dripped onto his clothes. A beautiful spicy, fruity smell filled the room.

Jesus' friends were surprised. They knew that the bottle of perfume must have cost a lot of money. Usually you just use the tiniest drop of perfume, but this woman had emptied the whole bottle onto Jesus!

'What a waste!' said Jesus' friends to each other. 'Instead of pouring the perfume over Jesus' head, she could have given it to us. Then we could have sold it and given the money to people who are poor. They could have used it to buy food. That would have been a much better thing to do.'

Jesus looked at his friends. He knew what they were talking about.

'This woman has done something really lovely,' he told them. 'She had a bottle of beautiful perfume that cost her a lot of money. But she has given it all to me as a very special present. Don't worry. There will be other times when you can help poor people. What this woman has done has made me very happy.'

The woman gave Jesus the perfume to show how much she loved him. Jesus said that people would always remember her and what she had done. And he was right, wasn't he? We're remembering today that she gave a special gift to Jesus!

Rhyme time

A special bottle

Read the rhyme through once. Read again, and ask the children to listen out for each time you say 'bottle': they then chant 'the very special bottle'. Practise this a couple of times and then say the rhyme again.

A woman had a bottle,
  a very special bottle,
And in that bottle,
  the very special bottle,
Was some perfume.
The woman took the bottle,
  the very special bottle,
And poured the perfume over Jesus.
Jesus' friends knew the bottle,
  the very special bottle,
Had cost the woman lots of money.
They could have sold the bottle,
  the very special bottle,
And given the money to poor people.
But Jesus said the bottle,
  the very special bottle,
Was a present that made him happy.
Yes, Jesus said the bottle,
  the very special bottle,
Was a present that made him happy.

Sing or say 'Mary's gift', *LACH*, p57.

Song time

At Simon's house

This song is to the tune of 'Do you know the muffin man?' Hold hands and skip in a circle while you sing the first verse; change directions between each verse.

Have you been to Simon's house,
Simon's house, Simon's house?
Have you been to Simon's house?
He lives in Bethany.

Jesus and his friends were there, . . .
There, in Bethany.

Did you see the woman there? . . .
There, in Bethany?

She came to Jesus with a gift, . . .
There, in Bethany.

She poured perfume on his hair, . . .
There, in Bethany.

Pray time

Gifts for Jesus

We can't give Jesus bottles of perfume and children can't give anything expensive: so what can they bring as gifts to Jesus? This active prayer will help them. You may wish to change the wording to 'we' instead of 'I' throughout.

I love Jesus. What gift can I bring?
I have a mouth, I have a voice,
Listen to me sing!
(Sing 'lah' to a favourite tune.)

I love Jesus, he loves me too.
He gave me fingers, he gave me hands.
See what I can do.
(Clap a simple rhythm.)

I love Jesus, what gift can I give?
He gave me legs, he gave me feet.
I can dance for him!
(Join hands and dance around in a circle together.)

We love Jesus. We bring our gifts for him.
We love Jesus! Jesus is our king!
(Lah, clap and dance.)

Extra time

- Make fancy and exotic looking jars and pots from play dough.
- Ask the children if they have a special treasure. Things don't have to be expensive to be special to us.
- Decorate empty plastic bottles with paint and glitter, or paste on pieces of paper to give a mosaic effect.

Adults too

Unlike our perfume bottles today, there was no replaceable lid on the bottle in the story. You literally broke the top off the bottle, to release the exotic pure nard, an eastern spicy perfumed oil, so expensive that a woman would have saved it for her wedding. Yet Jesus valued the woman's gift for the beauty and extravagance of her action. What do we really value in life? Introduce this topic in a non-threatening way by playing a light-hearted game: assuming the people and pets are safe, what three things would you rescue from a burning building? Often it's not things of monetary value that are worth most to us: most people choose personal items – photos, an ancient teddy bear, a faded menu from that special hotel…

If appropriate, lead on to showing how the values that Jesus showed in his life and teaching led to his death: he turned the ways of his world inside out and people loved him – and hated him – for doing so.

Top tip

'Bethany' is a popular girls' name: do make sure the children know what you're talking about when you mention the name as a town in this session!

Begin a 'bits' box at your group for useful items for craft and modelling activities. Encourage people to donate any old magazines (with suitable pictures), yoghurt pots, cardboard tubes, egg boxes, newspapers, etc. Make specific requests on your notice board or newsletter for unusual items or particular toys.

ACTIVITY PAGE:
The photocopiable activity page for this outline is on page 19

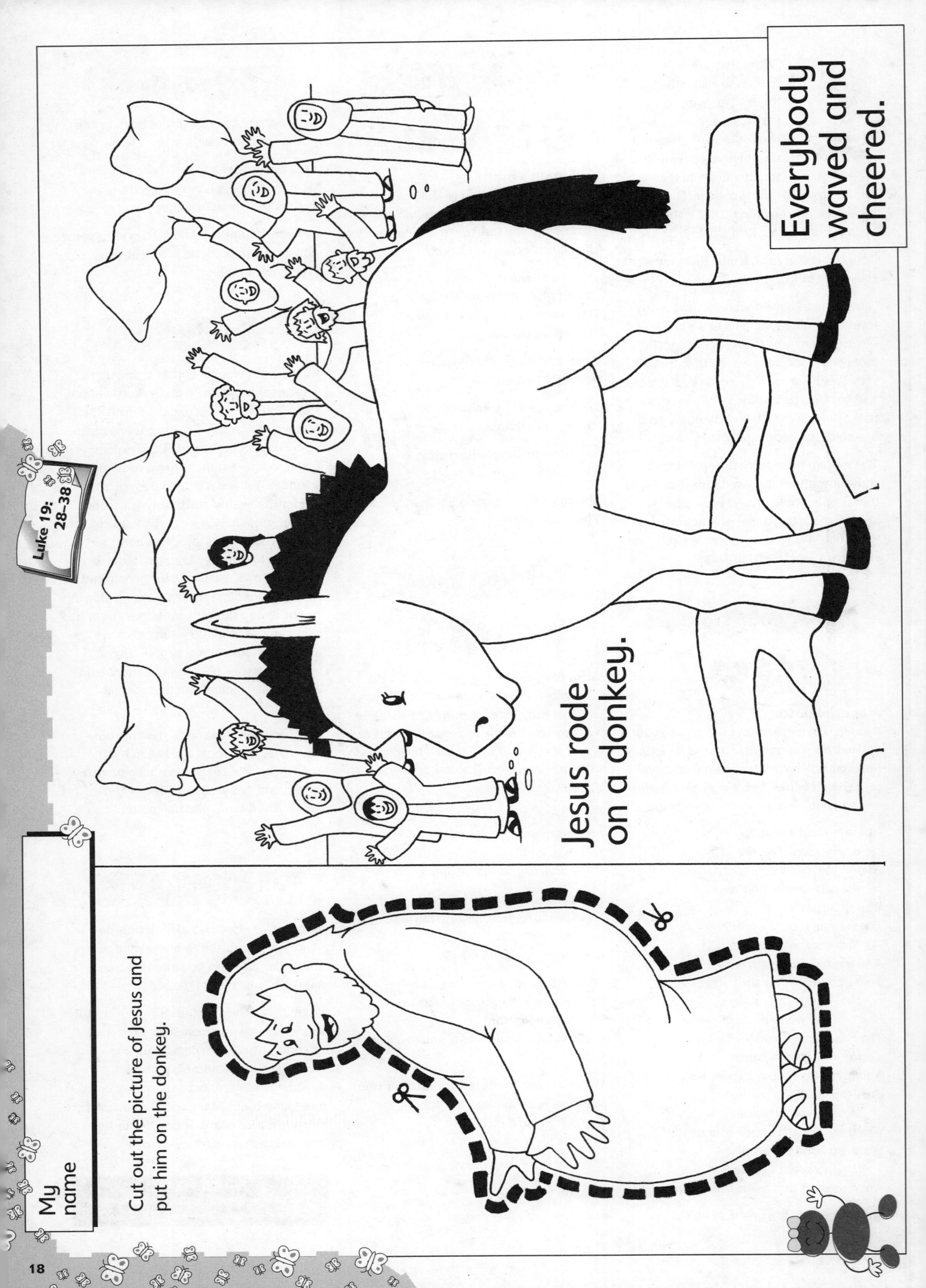

3 Easter
Supper time

Luke 22: 7–20

Play time
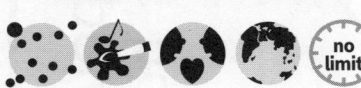

Kitchen play
Set out a kitchen corner with plenty of toys to encourage children to prepare a meal for their friends. What are their favourite foods? How does it look? Will it be really special? Encourage the children to treat each other or the dolls and soft toys to a tea party.

Construction play
Put out building blocks and suggest the children use them to make houses. Give some assistance to children in building a first-century house: add a large upstairs room and include a table. How is this house different from our homes? Do we usually have rooms for eating in, upstairs?

Bread
Prepare some bread dough in advance. Each child will need enough to make a medium-sized bread roll. Allow the children to complete the final kneading, and to shape their bread. Encourage them to make it fairly flat and round, just like the bread that Jesus ate. (Your bread will still rise.) Bake the bread during the session so that it is ready to take home. Be alert to hygiene, safety and the possibility of allergies; keep children away from cooking areas.

Lay the table
Give each child a plate, fork and spoon (real, play ones or card cut-outs). Let them organise these on a table, ready for a meal. If you have adults staying, ask them to join in and show the children how they lay the table at their homes (you may get many different arrangements).

Dough play
Encourage children to make some food items out of play or salt dough. Chat with them about what they are making: what are their favourite foods? What would they like to eat at a party? What do they like for their dinner? If you are using salt (baking) dough, cook the food shapes and use them for home and shop play.

Game time

Apples and oranges
You will need: an apple and orange (plastic or real), and at least two leaders.

Play for fun, not as a race. Divide the children into two groups, and sit them on the floor in two lines, facing each other. Clear a large space around each row. Give the apple to the first child in one row and the orange to the other. The children must pass the fruit down their row, from hand to hand; the child at the end must run back to the top with the fruit to pass it down again. When the original children are back at the top of the lines the game is over.

How about refreshing everyone with a drink of apple or orange juice?

Making time

Bread basket
You will need: squares of card approx 20 cm, strips of card 20 x 4 cm, scissors, sticky tape, self-adhesive shapes, napkins.

Fold and cut the card square as shown.

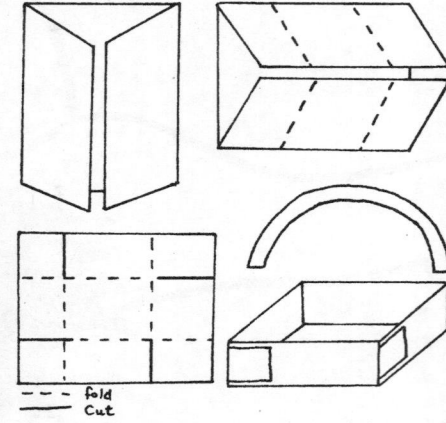

Write the child's name on a strip of card and tape this on as a handle.

Encourage the children to decorate their baskets with the shapes. Place a napkin in the base of the basket and then put in their bread roll, if you made it today, or play dough shapes.

Story time

Jesus' last meal
You will need: bread (pitta, chapatti, naan), diluted grape or blackcurrant juice, cups.

Share out the bread and drink during the Bible story. Two versions are given below, use the one which suits your group.

Short version: Jesus knew he was going to leave his friends. He knew his friends would be sad. So Jesus wanted to have a special meal with them so that he could say, 'Goodbye. Don't forget me.' All Jesus' best friends came to the meal and they sat in a big room to eat together.

Jesus gave his friends some bread. 'When you eat bread like this, remember me,' he said.

Jesus gave his friends a drink. 'When you drink like this, remember me,' he said.

Longer version: Jesus asked Peter and John to get everything ready for a special last meal together. 'Go to the city,' he told them, 'and look for a man carrying a water pot. He will show you where we are going to have our meal.'

Peter and John found the man and he took them to his house. It had a big room upstairs. Peter and John got everything ready for the meal. That evening, Jesus and his friends came to dinner. They all sat down. Everyone looked at Jesus.

Jesus smiled. 'I've been looking forward to sharing this meal with you,' he told his friends. 'I have to do something very hard, something that God wants me to do. I will have to leave you for a while.'

Jesus' friends felt sad. They didn't want Jesus to go away.

Jesus took the bread *(demonstrate)* and used his fingers to break it into pieces. 'Look,' he said gently, 'my body will be broken just as I've broken the bread. When you eat the bread, it will help you to remember me.' Jesus gave each of his friends a piece of bread.

Jesus picked up the drink. 'When you

Remember me
Music by Elizabeth Hume

Je-sus said, "Re-mem-ber me!" Je-sus said, "Re-mem-ber me!" Je-sus said, "Re-mem-ber me! Re-mem-ber that I love you!"

© Scripture Union 2002

drink together,' he explained, 'it will help you remember me. You will be glad because I'm doing what God wants me to do. I am doing it because I love you.'

Jesus' friends all had some of the drink. They felt sad and a bit puzzled by it all. But they would not be sad for long. Some sad things would happen to Jesus, but he would come back again, and they would all be happy again.

Rhyme time

Think of Jesus
Even very young children can join in with this brief meditation. Play some quiet background music and sit the children round a low table. Place something on the table as a focus to look at, perhaps a plate of fresh bread or (with a lot of care) a lighted candle in a shielded holder. Invite the children to think about Jesus and how much he loves them. (Explain that 'wine' is a drink made from grape juice.) Say, clearly but quietly:

Jesus shared the bread, *(repeat)*
'When you meet together,
Remember me,' he said.

Jesus shared the wine, *(repeat)*
'Don't forget: remember
That you are friends of mine.'

You may wish to end this quiet time by joining hands and saying this prayer, with everyone echoing each phrase after you,
'Lord Jesus, thank you for being our friend. Help us to remember you.'

Song time

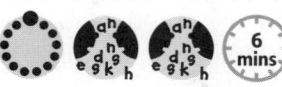

Jesus said
To encourage the children to use their memories, play 'Kim's game'. Put about ten items on a tray; let the children look at it for a minute; then either discreetly remove one item and let the children work out which is missing; or cover the tray and encourage them to remember all the items. Praise their memory skills and say that Jesus wanted his friends to remember him. One way he did that was to have a special meal with them. This song helps us remember what he said. Sing it through several times to help you all remember the song. The music is at the top of the page.

Jesus said, 'Remember me', *(repeat twice)*
'Remember that I love you.'

Ask, 'What did Jesus ask us to remember?'

Pray time

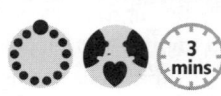

To Jesus
Use the rhyme time meditation or lead this prayer, with everyone joining in the response (shown in italics).

Lord Jesus, you came from heaven above.
We thank you, Jesus.

You came to tell of God's great love.
We thank you, Jesus.

You came to teach us how to live.
We thank you, Jesus.

You came to show us how to give.
We thank you, Jesus.

Lord Jesus we want you to know…
We thank you, Jesus.
We will follow where you go.

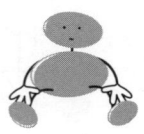

Extra time

- Sample different types of bread: naan, pitta or matzos are unleavened, like the bread used at the Passover meal. Make toast or toasted sandwiches: let them cool before eating. Check on allergies and avoid products containing whole grains or nuts, for this age group.

- Cut out pictures of food from magazines and stick them on to paper plates to make your own feast.

- Serve red-coloured fruit drinks and small sandwiches for your refreshments today.

Adults too

Invite parents and carers to join you in a Passover meal. This can be during or after your usual session and include the children, or you might like to make it a separate event, giving you more opportunity to get to know one another in a social setting. Passover was a serious event and the type of food eaten may not seem very much like a 'party'!

To hold an authentic Jewish seder meal with Christian interpretation, read *Passover Haggadah*, from Purple Pomegranate Productions available through 'Jews for Jesus' (www.jfjonline.org).

Top tip

A feature of the Jewish meal is the opportunity for the younger members of the group to ask questions which the older ones answer: use this idea to talk about the events of Easter, making sure that the children are assured that Jesus is alive.

Several of the activities in this session involve eating and drinking: for any item involving food, safety and hygiene issues and check with parents and carers about possible allergies. Keep note of these in your records and plan to avoid products which might affect children in the group.

ACTIVITY PAGE:
The photocopiable activity page for this outline is on page 24

4 Easter
Good Friday

Play time

Dead or alive?
You will need: a selection of seeds, bulbs, dried flowers, dead twigs, a dead pot plant to introduce the idea of death and dying; equipment for growing cress.

Let the children touch and talk about the plant material. Why do cut-flowers die so quickly? Because they have been taken off the plant which is alive. Some plants die at the end of a season, or because they have not had water. But plants make seeds and bulbs. Look at some seeds: they seem dry and dead, but they can grow into new green living plants!

Give each child a clean half egg shell, or yoghurt pot, and cotton wool. Help them to fill the pot with cotton wool, water it and then sprinkle on cress seeds. Explain how to keep the cotton wool moist and to watch what happens to the dry dull-looking seed over the next few days.

Easter scene
Make a Good Friday garden. Use a sand tray or shallow box, filled with play sand or clean compost. Shape a hill at one end of the tray and a cave-tomb at the other. Make pathways of small stones. Use a larger flat stone to go over the cave opening. Make three crosses from twigs or craft sticks: press these into the hill.

Free style
Set out paints and paper in sombre colours (purples, greys, deep blues and dull reds) for children to use to express sad or serious feelings. Try to make time to talk to children about their artwork: don't be too quick to cheer them up, but let them use their creativity and their words to express sad feelings.

Game time

I am alive
With children facing you, explore our five senses, each time declaring, 'I am alive!' or 'We are alive!' (Be sensitive to children with impairments to any of their senses.).

Say: 'Touch your nose! Can you smell? *(Breathe in through your nose.)* What can you smell?' *(Ask children to respond with what their senses are telling them.)* 'I am alive!'

Continue: 'Can you feel your hands? *(Touch different textures.)* 'I am alive!'

'Where are your eyes? What can you see? Cover your eyes. What can you see? Open your eyes.' 'I am alive!' 'Put your finger on your tongue. What do you like to taste with your tongue?' 'I am alive!' 'Touch your ears. What can you hear?' 'I am alive!'

Making time

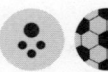 

Look at the cross
This paper tearing activity is easier than it sounds! Go through slowly and clearly step-by-step, giving children plenty of time to copy your actions and helping them as necessary; children as young as three can cope with this and they love the surprise result!

Use a rectangle of lightweight paper (A4 size is ideal).

1 Fold top left-hand corner over to meet the right-hand edge of the paper.

2 Fold top point of the triangle across to bottom-left point.

3 Fold in half.

4 Fold in half lengthways.

5 From the middle of the square end, tear in half.

6 Open out the largest piece to see the cross!

Bookmarks
Children can decorate cross-shaped bookmarks with crayons or adhesive shapes. Cover the finished picture with adhesive film, to protect book pages. Punch a hole at the top and loop thin ribbons through, to dangle from the book and mark the place.

Story time

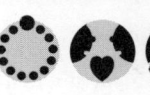

Good Friday
Create a safe and secure atmosphere for this quiet and sad story. Encourage the children to snuggle up with cushions and throws, or if possible, with their parents and carers. It's easy to make young children upset so be extra-sensitive in your storytelling and be sure to end on a positive note.

A few days before Good Friday, Jesus had ridden into the big city on a donkey. The people had clapped and cheered him. It had been very exciting.

But then a few days later, some men who did not like Jesus arranged for soldiers to take him away. The soldiers came one night when Jesus was in a large garden, praying with his friends. Jesus had not done anything wrong, but the soldiers made him a prisoner.

There was nothing that his friends could do to help him. They were very frightened. They did not know why Jesus had been taken away.

Then they heard that Jesus had died. Jesus had been killed by being nailed to a big wooden cross. Jesus, their friend, was dead! Jesus' friends were very, very sad. It seemed as if the whole world was sad. It was the middle of the afternoon but the sun stopped shining and it went very dark.

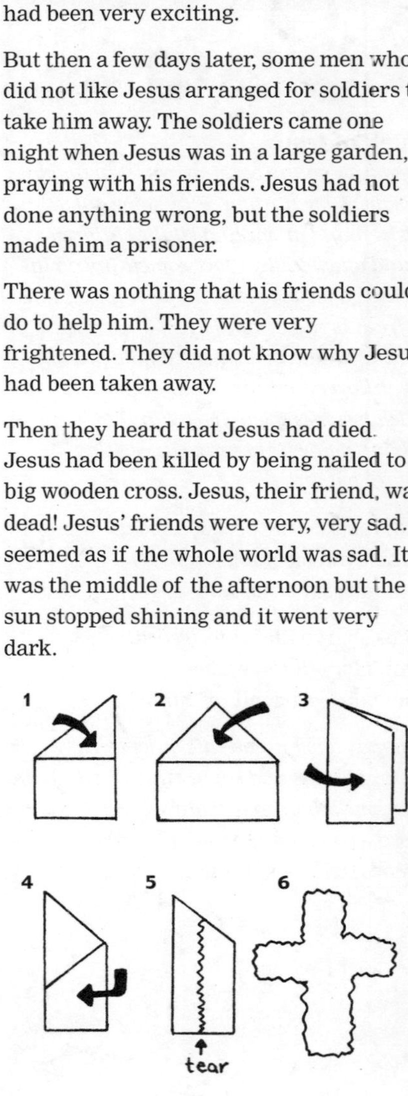

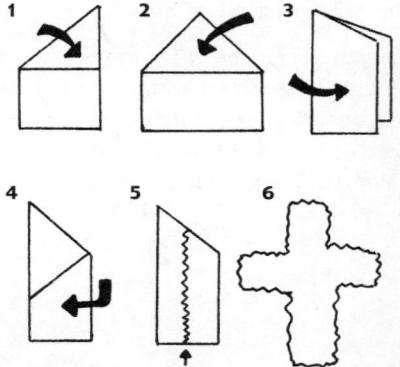

Jesus' friends took his dead body down from the big wooden cross. They wrapped him up in a long white cloth and took him to a cave. It was a tomb or grave, a place where Jesus' body would stay.

Gently, they laid Jesus' body down in the cave. There wasn't a door so they rolled a big stone across the way in. They said 'goodbye' to Jesus and went away. They were very sad and very afraid. Their best friend Jesus was dead. He was no longer with them to help them. They would miss him so much. They thought they would never see him again.

But they were wrong!

They would be seeing Jesus again. Very soon!

God was about to do something very wonderful indeed. In just a few days' time, God would bring Jesus back to life again!

Rhyme time

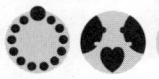   

Good Friday?
Children often ask what is so good about Good Friday. Agree that it is a strange name for a sad day. But explain that we know something that Jesus' friends didn't know on that day: Jesus was made alive again by God. When Jesus died, he took away the blame for all the wrong and naughty things that we've done so that we can be friends with God. What happened was sad, but we can look back and say thank you to God for Jesus.

Sad Friday, sad Friday,
Oh what a sad day,
Jesus died on the cross,
Oh what can we say?

Long Friday, long Friday,
His friends are all sad,
But a happy day is coming,
And then they'll be glad.

Good Friday? Good Friday!
That's what we say.
Jesus is alive again!
Thank you, God! Hooray!

Song time

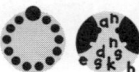

Hot cross buns
You will need: either one bun as an example or enough to share.

Sing the traditional rhyme 'Hot cross buns'. Ask if anyone knows what a hot cross bun looks like? It's 'cross' because there are lines on the top forming the shape of a cross. Show an example and let the children trace the pattern with their fingers (this won't be one to eat!). Explain that people make and eat this type of bun to remind them about Jesus being put on the cross on Good Friday. Sing the song again and add this verse:

Jesus died, Jesus died,
But the happy news we share is –
He's alive!

Pray time

How we feel
This prayer can also be sung, if you know the nursery tune of 'I like peace, I like quiet'. Sit in a circle, with arms folded and heads down. Say or sing twice:

I feel sad, I feel sorry, Jesus died upon the cross.

Then change the mood by standing up, clapping and dancing as you say or sing twice:

I feel great, I feel happy, Jesus is alive again.

Extra time

- 'Jesus is the son of God', *LSS*, p63.
- 'Sing a song', *KS* 297.
- Look at the story of Good Friday in an illustrated children's Bible (making sure you continue the story to the happy events of Easter day).

Adults too

This session may stir up reactions in the children or it may stimulate adults to think about how a child copes with death. Understanding children's grief and helping them handle situations of loss often leaves us confused ourselves. Often we can (wrongly) jump to the conclusion that children aren't grieving because they don't handle their grief in the same way as we do. When young children face a difficult challenge they generally handle it in small chunks, naturally sensing when they are no longer able to concentrate adequately on the task. It seems they handle grief in this way too. When the pain is too overwhelming they will turn their attention to something else for a while. Realising this, we must not underestimate the intensity of the child's grieving. We need to be there respectfully – a comforting presence, reflecting the child's feelings, helping them to realise that in time the sad feelings won't feel so strong, answering questions and, when appropriate, remembering happy times.

(From *Tiddlywinks: My Little Yellow Book*)

Recommended reading: *Children and Grieving*, Janet Goodall, SU.

Top tip

A child's understanding of death is not the same as that of an adult. It will be several more years before they can start to grasp the full reality of death and its permanency. This gives us peculiar challenges as we introduce the death of Jesus: young children will be sad about the events, the unfairness of it and the way he died (it's not helpful to dwell on these in too much detail). The wonder of the resurrection is almost an anti-climax for most young children. When you don't understand that death is permanent, you're not surprised when someone comes back to life! At the same time, it's important that children leaving the session today are assured that the story doesn't end with Jesus' death, that he does come back to life again and that the story does have a happy ending.

ACTIVITY PAGE:
The photocopiable activity page for this outline is on page 25

Copy or mount the page on to card; cut out and assemble the model if you have time, so that children can use it straight away to tell each other the story.

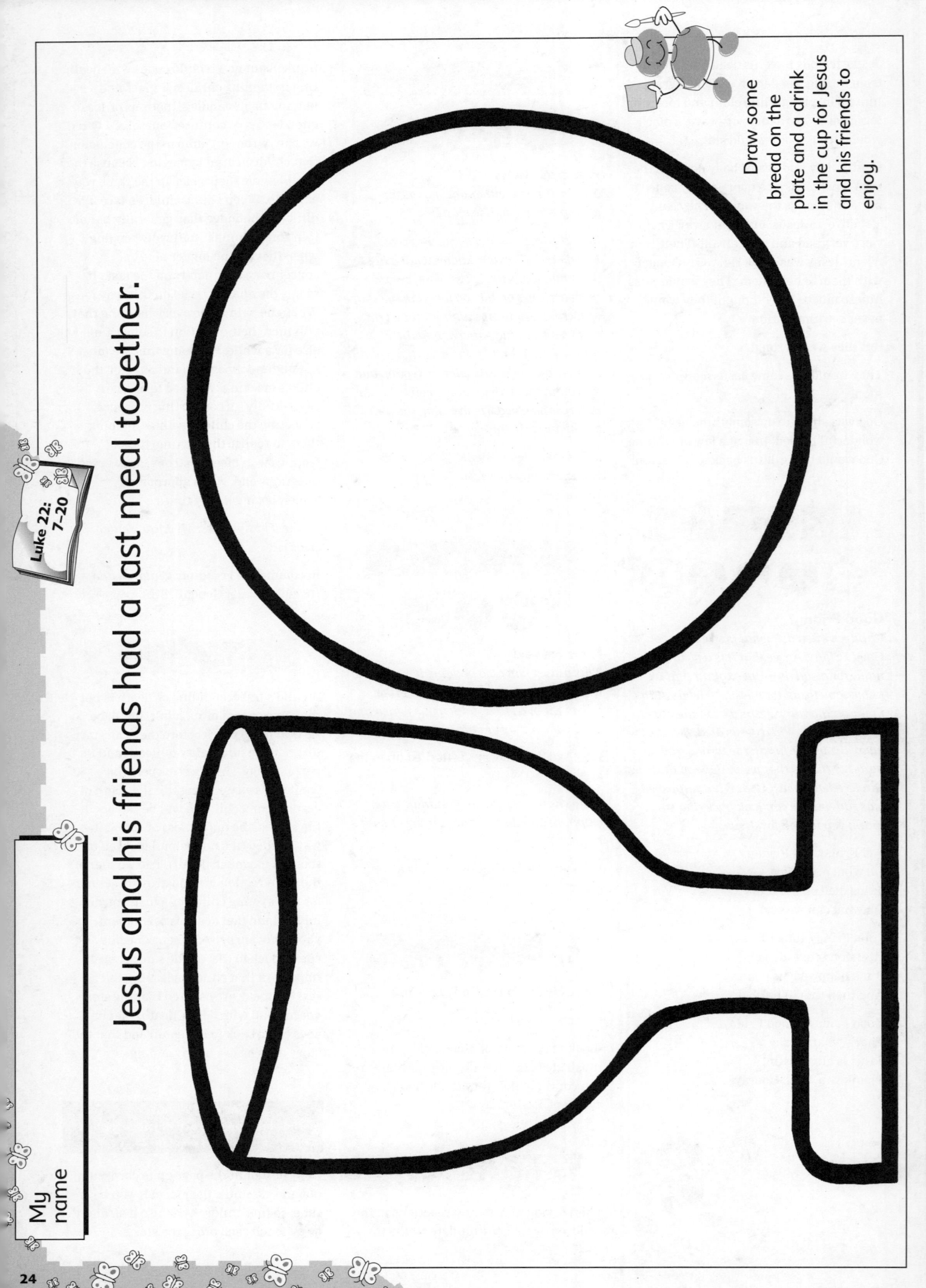

Jesus died but God brought him back to life again!

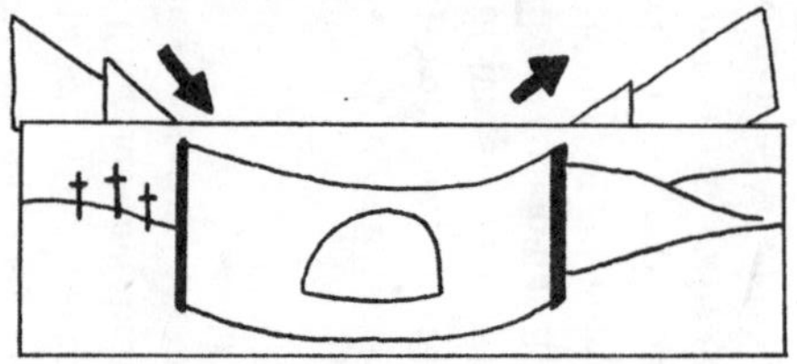

My name

Mark 15

Cut slits in the garden scene as shown. Cut away the entrance to the cave. Use the spare strips of card to make handles either side of the small scenes. Thread through the slits. Pull the handle and tell the story.

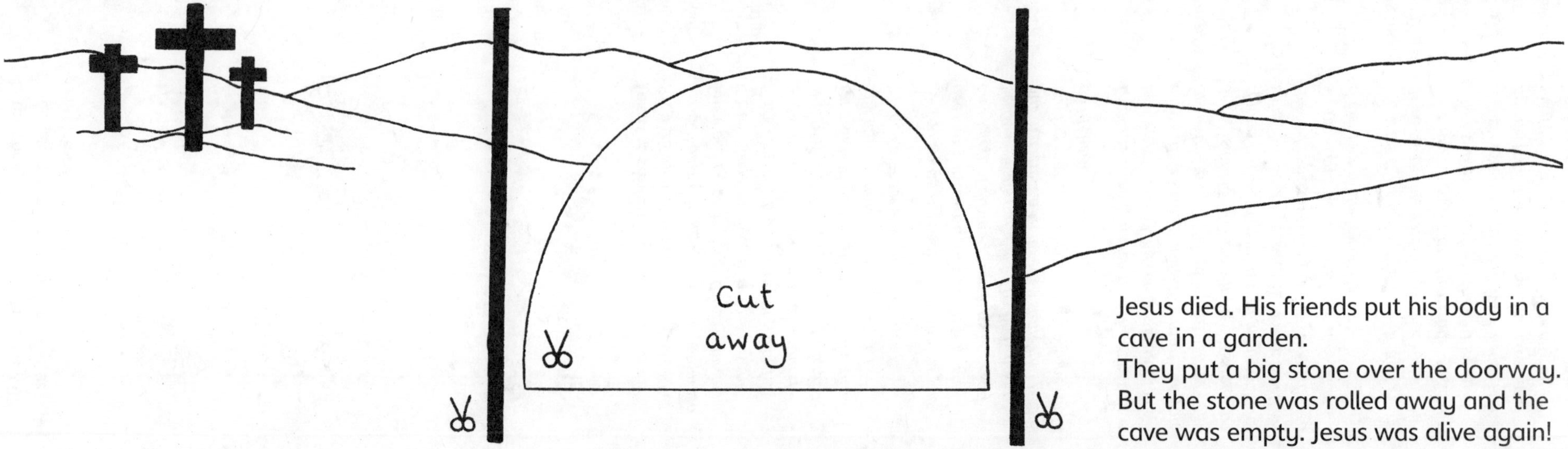

Jesus died. His friends put his body in a cave in a garden. They put a big stone over the doorway. But the stone was rolled away and the cave was empty. Jesus was alive again!

25

5 Easter
Jesus is alive!

Luke 24: 1–12

Play time

These ideas will help children experience the fun of being alive. Some activities will need adult guidance and direction but all can be included in an informal play session.

Move it!
Sing and do the actions to 'Head, shoulders, knees and toes' or a similar nursery song. How many ways of working our bodies can you think of, as you play 'Here we go round the mulberry bush'? Breathe in and out through your mouth; and then your nose. Count out loud to five, clapping hands the right number of times. Are we alive? Yes we are because we can breathe, move and make a noise!

Tumbling tots
Lay out padded floor mats and let children practise their exercises. Star jumps, rolling sideways, bunny hops are all safe and easy to do. Are we alive? Yes we are!

Sort it!
Set out a collection of items and ask the children to sort them into two groups: things which are alive and things which are not alive. You could include: a plastic insect/a live insect in a container (to be liberated later); a live pot plant/a dried flower; a doll/a baby (with carer!). Are we alive? Yes we are – so which group would we be in?

Blow!
Stand the children in a row and ask them to put a hand on their tummies and take a deep breath. Can they feel the change as the air goes into their bodies? Let the breath out again: how did that feel? Chat about breathing air in and out of our lungs: would we be able to breathe if we were not alive? Are we alive? Blow and feel the air on the back of your hand. Yes we are!

Game time

Fun with feathers
You will need: clean feathers at least 10 cm long (available from craft shops).

Limit the number of feathers in use at one time and supervise carefully to make sure they are played with safely. Put a feather on one side of a low table: ask how to get it to the other side without touching it. Try any methods suggested but settle on 'blowing'. Blow the feather across the table. Give several children feathers and let them try: don't make this into a race – they will have fun just blowing. Develop the game by setting up simple goals, etc.

Egg hunt
Easter eggs are symbols that every child will recognise – though they may not know why! Prepare an egg hunt, using small chocolate eggs or cardboard ones decorated with wrapping paper. If the hunt is not in your usual meeting area, make sure all children are accompanied as they search.

Making time

Easter chicks
You will need: pom-pom circles cut beforehand, plenty of yellow wool, sharp scissors for adult use.

Guide the children as they wind wool to make a pom-pom. For younger children, have the wool partly wound round so the card circles do not slip. When the winding is complete, cut the loops and tie very tightly in the middle before removing the card. Fluff up the pom-pom and hand to the child. Talk about how soft and fluffy it feels, just like a new-born chick. Have they seen chicks on Easter cards? They are baby birds, all fresh and new and alive. They help us remember the new life of Jesus at Easter.

(If you wish, you can add eyes and a beak to the pom-pom, but most children will use their imaginations and look after their 'chick' as it is.)

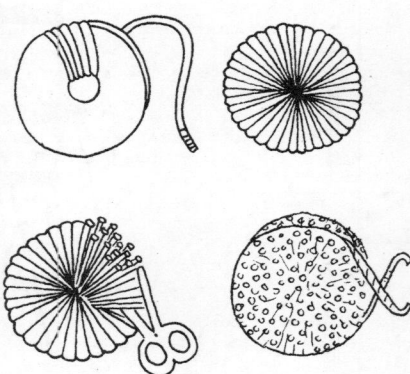

Story time
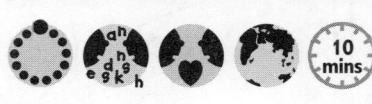

Jesus is alive!
Prepare some improvised scenery: a sheet draped over a table to be the cave-tomb, a large bean bag as the entrance stone. Get the children involved in acting out the story, as you tell it in your own words. Enter into this enthusiastically and the children will quickly follow your lead. Include and involve all the children and any willing adults, taking the parts of the women who went to the garden.

As you set up the scene, explain that you are going to hear about the first Easter day. On that day everyone was very sad because Jesus had died. His body had been put in a cave. And a heavy stone had been put in front of the cave so that no one could go in there.

Explain to the children that they are going to pretend to be friends of Jesus and to be very sad. It's early in the morning and you are going to visit the cave-tomb where Jesus is buried. (Some simple dressing-up clothes will help the children get into their roles, but are not essential. Do not dwell on the sad aspects of the story too long: aim to set the scene, put the events in context but then move to the joy of Easter.)

Walk together to your cave-tomb and discover that the stone has been rolled away (arrange for another leader to do this while you are talking to the children). Express your surprise that the heavy stone has been moved. Look into the 'cave' and see that Jesus' body isn't there any more. Look all around. Ask 'Where has he gone'?

26

Look surprised again as you suddenly 'see' two bright lights by the cave. (Pretend there are two bright angels there.) Hide your eyes, crouch on the floor. Ask the children to listen – the angels are speaking to you. Say that they are telling you all not to be afraid or worried. 'Listen' again and 'repeat' their words to the children: the angels are saying that Jesus is not in the cave-tomb anymore because he's alive again! Be amazed! Be excited and happy! Say that Jesus is alive again! Shout 'Hooray! Jesus is alive!' together.

(If you wish, extend the drama to going and telling Peter and the other followers, and passing the wonderful news on to them.)

Rhyme time

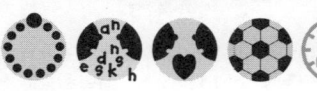

Jesus is alive
A clapping rhyme, with five claps to each line. Start up the clapping rhythm:

Clap, clap, clap-clap, clap.

The children will soon copy the beat; then overlay the clapping with the rhyme words. Repeat several times, so the children can gradually start to join in with the words too.

'Jesus is alive', *(repeat)*
All the children cry,
'Jesus is alive!'

'Jesus is our friend, *(repeat)*
His love never ends,
Jesus is our friend.'

Also:

'Easter morning', *LACH*, p68
'Hooray!' *LSS*, p63
'Jesus is alive', *LSS*, p61

Song time

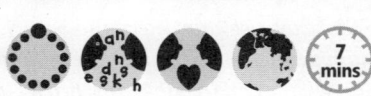

This song tells the story to the tune of 'The wheels on the bus'. If the children have not already heard the word 'tomb', explain that it to them. The women were going there to say a last goodbye to Jesus – but he wasn't there because God had brought him to life again. Jesus is alive!

The women were sad when Jesus died,
Jesus died, Jesus died,
The women were sad when Jesus died,
Jesus died.

The women went down to Jesus' tomb…
On Easter day.

What a surprise! He wasn't there!…
On Easter day!

Jesus is alive today…
On Easter day!

Jesus is with us all day long…
Every day!

Also:

'Jesus is alive', *LACH*, p71

Pray time

Easter shout!
Explain that as we're so happy that it's Easter and that Jesus is alive, we're going to make lots of noise to show how excited we are. Before you go any further, teach a signal for 'stop'. Then let the children clap, shout 'hooray', jump and use musical shakers and jingle bells to help them praise God. Join in to show that being noisy and happy in this way is allowed. Encourage children who are wary, by staying close to them and joining in at the edge of the main group. Give your 'stop' signal and then lead a praise shout, with the children echoing each phrase after you:

Jesus is alive today.
Hooray, hooray!
He is with us every day.
Hooray, hooray!

End by marching round the room, dropping the instruments into a storage box as you pass by. Emphasise that Jesus is pleased to hear the children's praise.

Extra time

•Read *The First Easter* (Bible Pebbles series, SU).

•Pass the egg! Pass a wrapped Easter egg round the circle while the music plays. When the music stops, the child holding the egg keeps it and everyone shouts 'Hooray, Jesus is alive!' Use another egg to play again: continue till everyone has an egg. (Once you have an egg, you can still play but you only keep one!)

•Go for a walk, with plenty of adult supervision, and enjoy all the things you see and hear that are alive.

•Break clean eggshells into pieces, colour these with food colouring and use to make colourful mosaic pictures.

Adults too

God created life and God raised Jesus from the dead. Prepare a short talk on what it means to be a Christian. Focus in on the gospel message, showing that Jesus died for each of the adults and children in your group. Practise what you are going to say so that you can express yourself in a clear and loving way, without making your listeners feel uncomfortable. Jesus' death on the cross wasn't the end; it was just the beginning. God raised Jesus to life. We trust in a living God. Sometimes that can seem too easy or too hard! Have some practical, personal (and recent) examples of when being a Christian has made a difference in your life.

Bring some seedling plants from the garden centre, along with compost and pots for replanting. Ask the adults if they would like to pot a plant to take home as an Easter gift. (You could have your discussion during this time.) Or present the adults with a gift of a young plant, representing new life, after your discussion.

Top tip

'It was Easter morning. "It's Easter! It's Easter!" shouted Danny. "Can I eat my Easter eggs now?!" he asked his mum.'

Tiddlywinks: My Little Yellow Book gives children their first steps in Bible reading, exploring the same stories that are in this book. For ordering information, see page 89 or 96. *My Little Books* are also available in value packs of 10: why not get some for the children and families in your group?

ACTIVITY PAGE:
The photocopiable activity page for this outline is on page 30

6 Easter
Easter day

Play time

Easter eggs

Draw large egg shapes on sheets of paper and let the children experiment with what to do with them. Provide art materials and guidance so they can:

- Colour or paint the shape in bright colours.

- Print Easter symbols (chick, cross, egg, flower) all over it. (Make printing shapes from foam or stiff card; add a clothes peg or a card-tab as a handle.)

- Cut the egg roughly in half; mount the pieces on a background page and add a chick coming from the egg (chicks could be drawn or cut from yellow paper or fur fabric).

- Collage on scraps of torn or crumpled paper.

Surprise!

Put various 'surprise' toys around the room where children can discover them and experiment with them. You could include: a jack-in-the-box, a set of Russian stacking dolls, a pop-up puppet.

Easter nests

Stir shreds of breakfast cereal into melted chocolate. When this is touch-cool, give each child a generous spoonful and let them mould it and press it together to make a nest; add a few mini Easter eggs. (Have an alternative for those who cannot eat chocolate.) Take usual hygiene, safety and allergy precautions and ensure the children wash their hands before and after!

Easter bop

Play lively happy music and let the children dance spontaneously. Some will be totally uninhibited; others will be more confident if you join in too.

Flower power

Provide flowers (fresh, artificial or home-made paper ones), greenery and unbreakable pots so that children can make their own flower arrangements. Making paper flowers could be an additional activity: see *Here's One I Made Earlier* (SU) for methods, and for other Easter crafts.

You could invite a skilled flower arranger to come and give the children a quick and easy-to-copy demonstration.

Game time

Chinese whispers

The traditional way of playing this game doesn't work well with young children but you can still play it as a 'pass a message' game. Sit in a circle and give a message to the child next to you: speak quietly but clearly. That child then turns to the one next to him and passes the message on; and so on, until the message comes back to you. Choose a child a few places further on to start the next message travelling round. Repeat four times, using messages about today's Bible story: each time, make your voice a bit louder and a bit more excited.

1. Mary was sad.
2. Jesus had died.
3. Mary was happy.
4. Jesus is alive!

Egg hunt

A game for the end of the session. Prepare a 'nest' (a laundry basket) with a bag of chocolate Easter eggs, hidden by some shredded paper. Hide lots of colourful card egg shapes around the room, plenty for everyone to find. Let the children go and find them and bring them to you. Let them put the eggs into the 'nest'. When all the eggs have been found, reach into the nest and 'discover' the chocolate eggs hiding there: share them round!

Making time

Easter trees

You will need: a piece of play dough pressed into a plastic tub, a branching twig, lots of card egg shapes, shiny ribbon.

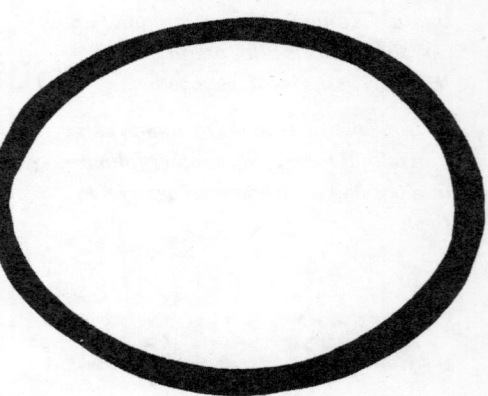

A traditional Easter decoration idea from Sweden. This could be an activity for the whole group or each child could make their own. Push the branching twig into the play dough in the tub. Decorate the card egg shapes and hang them from the twigs, with the ribbon. Add a ribbon bow to the tub and a label saying 'Jesus is alive!'

Story time

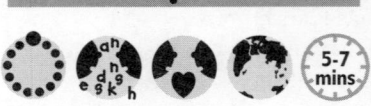

Mary meets Jesus

Draw a face on each thumb, one for Mary and one for Jesus. Using an elastic band, attach a scrap of material to make suitable clothing. Bend the thumb that is 'talking'. You could make some garden scenery out of a piece of card. Lean it against your lap and hold your thumbs up in front of it as you tell the story. Settle the children so they can see what you are doing. For a large group, use hand puppets so they can all see the action easily.

Introduce the two characters and briefly explain what they are going to be talking about: tell the children the story briefly in your own words which you can then reinforce with the mini-drama. Use this time to explain the practicalities: what a 'tomb' is; why Jesus was there; why Mary wasn't expecting to see him.

Then use your thumb-people or puppets to act out this script: create different voices –

to help the children know which character is speaking and to hold their attention.

MARY: I'm so sad. On Friday Jesus, the best friend I ever had, died. We put him here in this garden tomb. I just don't understand. You see we thought that Jesus was special. That he was God's son. I don't know why he had to die. It was the worst day of my life. Now the tomb is empty, someone has taken him away. Ohhh… I'm so sad. *(Mary cries.)*

JESUS: What's the matter?

MARY: Oh! Are you the gardener? Please sir, if you have taken away my friend, please tell me where he is?

JESUS: Mary, don't you know me?

MARY: Jesus? Jesus! It's really you. You're alive, this is wonderful!

JESUS: Yes Mary, it's really me. Go and tell all my friends that I have come back to life, just as I said I would. Tell them I'll see them soon.

MARY: Oh Jesus, of course I will. I can't wait to see their faces! This is the best day of my life!

Little books for little hands: The First Easter *(Bible Pebbles)* and Jesus Lives *(Little Fish), both published by SU.*

Rhyme time

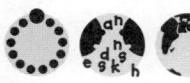

Mary meets Jesus
Explain that Mary was upset because she couldn't find Jesus. When she did find him, at first she thought he was someone working in the garden: then he spoke and she knew who he was. Mime actions, as suggested by the words.

Looking high, looking low,
Looking here and there,
Mary's looking for her friend,
She's looking everywhere.

Crying loud, crying long,
A gardener she can see.
'I am looking for my friend.
Wherever can he be?'

Happy smile, happy laugh,
'Mary,' he says, 'hello!'
Yes, it's Jesus: Mary says,
'You are alive I know!'

Song time

Poor Mary
If the children have not heard the story, explain briefly why Mary is 'a-weeping' (crying) and then play this ring game. The tune is 'Poor Jenny sits a-weeping'.

Choose a child to be 'Mary' and sit in the centre of the circle pretending to cry. Hold hands in the circle and stand still to sing:

Poor Mary is a-weeping, a-weeping, a-weeping,
Poor Mary is a-weeping, for she misses her friend.

'Mary' stands while everyone in the circle skips round singing:

But Jesus he is living…
On the first Easter day.

'Mary' joins the circle and all skip round together singing:

So Mary she is happy…
As we all are today.

Pray time

Good news
Focus on how we feel about Jesus being alive. It's good news and we can be very happy about it. Give the children crayons and a sheet of paper with a large circle drawn in the centre. Ask them to draw their face in the circle to show how they feel about Jesus being alive.

Hold up the faces so you can all see them and enjoy this praise shout. Say each line loudly and clearly; all repeat.

Jesus is alive today. *(repeat)*
He's with me in the night.
He's with me all the day.
Jesus is alive today!

Jesus wants to be my friend. *(repeat)*
Jesus never goes away.
His love will never end.
Jesus wants to be my friend.

Extra time

- Find more Easter rhymes in *Let's Sing and Shout!* and *Let's all Clap Hands!*, SU.
- Talk about being sad and happy. Pass round a cuddly toy: the child speaks when holding it. What things make the children happy or sad? Start by saying 'right now I feel…' Let the children discover ways of describing all sorts of feelings.
- Make hats or headbands on an Easter theme: hold an Easter bonnet parade just for fun!

Adults too

Make up a card for the adults with the word 'Reflections' as a heading. Print 'What makes me happy?' and leave a few lines underneath to write things down. Do the same for the phrase 'What makes me sad?' At the bottom of the card print 'How do I feel about God?' Many adults find it hard to talk about their feelings; some will not have asked the question about God. This is an opportunity to give the adults time to think.

If the adults know each other well and are comfortable together, you could adapt this into a 'consequences' game, passing the papers round between each question. Put all the completed papers in a heap and take them out one at a time and read them through aloud or pin them on a display board. Let comments and conversations arise naturally from this: leave space for people to mull over what they've written and what they've heard. (Destroy all papers afterwards.)

Top tip

Children do not have an understanding of death as being permanent: do not be surprised if their reaction to this most spectacular event is calm acceptance. They do not assume that being dead is a long-term state, so Jesus' resurrection is a happy event but not a remarkable one.

ACTIVITY PAGE:
The photocopiable activity page for this outline is on page 31

Fold the pages before you give them to the children so that only Mary is visible. Show them how to open out the page to make Jesus appear!

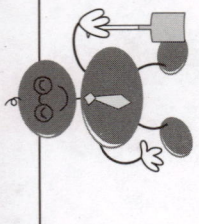

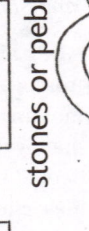 Luke 24: 1–12

Make an Easter garden.

My name

You will need:

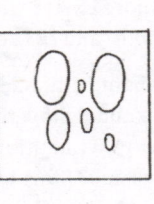 water

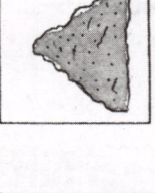 a shallow tray

 a short length of cardboard tube

 twigs

 moss

 small plants and flowers

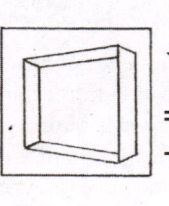 soil or sand

 stones or pebbles

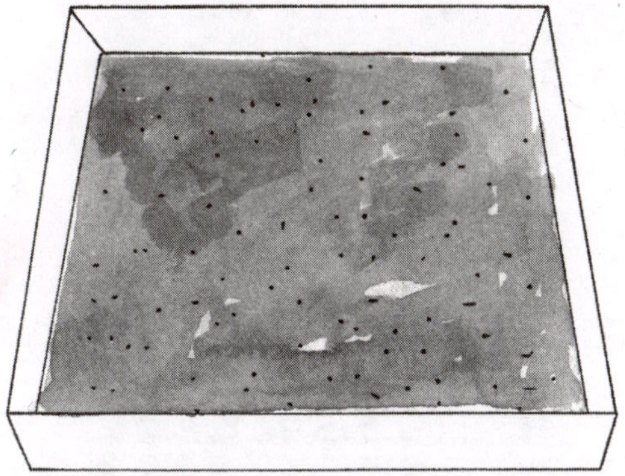

Put some soil in the tray. Spread it out.

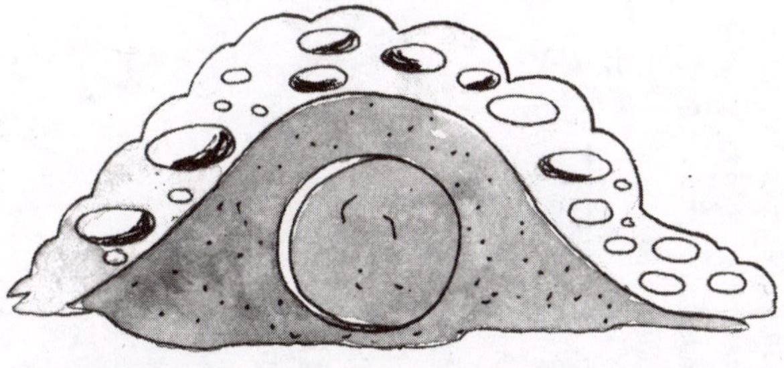

Put the tube in the tray and build a cave by covering it with soil and stones. Use a flat stone at the front as a door.

Push in some plants and add some twigs.

Water lightly.

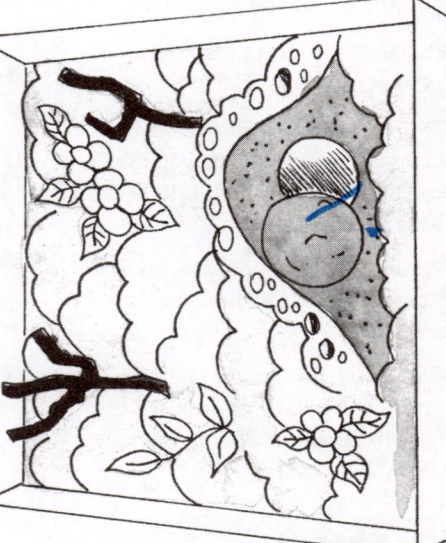

On Easter Day, take the door-stone away.

Jesus is alive!

7 Easter
On the road to Emmaus

Luke 24: 13–35

Play time

Go walkabout
If it is safe and practical to do so, go out together for a walk looking and listening as you go. (Make sure you have plenty of adult supervision and that carers and parents who are not staying, know what is happening.) If it's not possible to go outside, you could walk inside your building, imagining all the things you can see. When you return, sit and chat for a few minutes, about all the things you have seen and heard while you were out.

Spoon walking
Give each child a deep-bowled spoon and let them practise balancing a small potato or table tennis ball on it while they walk along. Don't race, just enjoy playing together and seeing how far and how quickly these pretend eggs can be carried.

Transport play
Set out vehicles, toy planes and road mats for children to play with. Join in and chat about going on journeys. Where are the cars going? Why are they going there? How long will it take? Discuss how the children came to the group today. Who came by car? Who walked? Who was in a buggy or on a bus? Arrange chairs to be different vehicles and let groups of children go for a journey. Spread out a piece of carpet and go for a flying carpet trip or ride a hobby-horse: where are you going? What will you see?

Game time

I walked like this…
How many variations on 'walking' can you think of? Run, stroll, trot? What others? Try out some ways – you can do some silly walks too!

Play the action game 'I went to school this morning', varying the way you 'walk' and putting in the name of your own group and time of meeting. (You'll probably need to stretch the tune to fit the name in.) So –

I went to 'Tiddlywinks' this morning and I *stepped* like this,
Stepped like this, *stepped* like this,
I went to 'Tiddlywinks' this morning and I *stepped* like this,
Step, step, step, step, step!

Start all lined up at one side of the room with a clear space in front of you. 'Walk' across the room during the verse; turn and come back using a different method of walking. Repeat several times with different ways.

Making time

Clay footprints
Children need to be able to take their own shoes and socks off (and put them on again!) or to have a parent or carer present to do this for them.

You will need: air-hardening clay, clay tools, greaseproof paper, a bowl of warm water, soap and a flannel. You will also need somewhere to place the casts until dry. (It can take from six to twenty-four hours to dry.)

For each footprint, you will need a lump of clay the size of two adult fists. Work the clay well and then shape it into a rectangle approximately 15 cm long x 10 cm wide x 2 cm deep, depending on the size of the child's foot. Place the clay onto greaseproof paper. Ask the child's carer to gently take the child's foot in their hands, and press the foot into the clay. With a clay tool write the name and the date into the clay.

Story time

On the road to Emmaus
Make large versions of these four faces; turn them face down in front of you. This story assumes Cleopas's companion was his wife: say 'Cleopas and his friend' if you prefer. Children will enjoy being 'in' on the fact that the man on the road is Jesus.

Mr and Mrs Cleopas, two friends of Jesus, were walking slowly along the road back to their home in the little village of Emmaus. They were very sad. *(Show saddest face.)* They thought that Jesus had died. But they didn't know that Jesus was alive again!

'Why did Jesus have to die?' sighed Cleopas.

'I miss him,' sighed Mrs Cleopas. 'He was such a good friend.'

Just then a man came walking along the road. 'What's the matter?' asked the man. 'Why do you look so sad?'

So they told him all about Jesus and why they were so unhappy.

'Don't be sad!' the man said. 'Jesus is alive! God has brought him back to life.' *(Less sad face.)*

They walked some more and the man talked some more. And as he talked, Mr and Mrs Cleopas felt a bit happier. *(Slightly happy face.)* They did not know it, but the man was Jesus! Soon they got to Mr and Mrs Cleopas's home in the little village of Emmaus. It was getting dark.

'Come in for something to eat,' Mrs Cleopas said to Jesus. Jesus went in with them. They still did not know who he was! Soon the food was ready. Jesus picked up the bread. He broke a piece off and said 'thank you' to God. Suddenly Mr and Mrs Cleopas knew who the man was! Who was he? Jesus!

'It's Jesus!' gasped Mr and Mrs Cleopas. 'He IS alive!' But by then, Jesus had left the house. *(Happy face.)*

Mr and Mrs Cleopas weren't sad any more. They wanted to tell all Jesus' other friends that he was alive. They ran out of the house. They ran all the way back along the road.

'Jesus is alive!' sang Mrs Cleopas, as she ran.

'Jesus is alive!' shouted Mr Cleopas, as they met Jesus' other friends. 'We've seen him. We've walked with him. We've talked with him. Jesus is alive!'

Rhyme time

He's alive!
This rhyme is 'spoken' by the friends of Jesus who met him on the road. Imagine you are waiting in Jerusalem and they have just run all the way back to tell you this!

We have seen him, he's alive,
We have seen him, he's alive,
We have seen him, he's alive,
Jesus is alive!

Jesus walked the road with us, *(x 3)*
We know he's alive!

He sat down to eat with us, *(x 3)*
So we know he's alive!

He will always be with us, *(x 3)*
Jesus is alive!

Song time

Two friends: two songs
This song is to the tune of 'The happy wanderer'. Walk around or on the spot as you sing. Children will soon be able to join in with the chorus and can have added fun by jingling bells or using shakers for these lines.

Jesus our friend is here with us,
Wherever we may go,
And we can walk and talk with him,
We know he loves us so.
He's alive! He's alive! He's alive! He's alive!
He's alive! He's alive! Our Jesus is alive!

And to the tune of 'Sing a song of sixpence' –

Two friends on a journey,
Heading back to home,
When a stranger joined them,
Asking what was wrong.
'Jesus died,' they told him.
'We don't understand.'
'Let me help you,' said the man,
As he told them God's plan.

Jesus was the stranger,
They saw when they got home.
Then he disappeared,
Leaving them alone,
But they understood now,
Why he had to die,
And best of all they knew for sure
That Jesus is alive!

Pray time

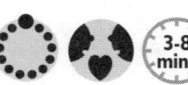

Along the road
The two friends talked to Jesus as they walked home, he listened to them and talked to them too. We can talk to Jesus as our friend, when we're walking or playing or in bed or whatever we're doing. Sing the song below to the tune of 'Bobby Shaftoe'. After each verse, pause to let the children talk to Jesus, aloud or in their heads.

We can always talk to Jesus,
We can always talk to Jesus,
We can always talk to Jesus,
And we know he listens.
(Pause to talk to Jesus.)

We can tell him how we're feeling…
And we know he listens.
(Pause to talk to Jesus.)

We can ask him to help others…
And we know he listens.
(Pause to talk to Jesus.)

Extra time

• *We're Going on a Bear Hunt*, Michael Rosen and Helen Oxenbury, Walker Books Ltd, or use the bear hunt formula for a game.

• Have a prayer walk: walk around the room and each time you stop, say a short prayer aloud.

• 'Two friends', p70, 'On Easter Day', p71, 'Jesus is alive' p71, *LACH*.

Adults too

In the Bible story, the travellers were literally on a journey, walking from one place to another. But what about the 'journey of life' that we are all on? Parents and carers of young children have few opportunities to think and reflect. Today, give out paper and pens (and boards to lean on) and suggest the adults draw a timeline of 'my life' with significant dates, events and people marked on. This can be kept as a personal interest or you could discuss the diagrams together in pairs or small groups. This need not become too heavy or serious but you may find it stimulates deeper questions and opens up opportunities to share your faith as you think about the key moments on your own journey.

Top tip

Fantasy play is important for young children. They are able to control situations, which helps build their confidence. They are able to act out their concerns, and even fears, in a safe way and find ways of handling situations. And fantasy play is great fun too! Encourage children to use and develop their imaginations in playing, art and problem-solving: as well as being significant learning skills, imagination and creativity give vibrancy to our faith.

ACTIVITY PAGE:
The photocopiable activity page for this outline is on page 36

8 Easter
A barbecue on the beach

John 21: 1–14

Play time

no limit

Have a barbecue
Mix real equipment and fantasy play to enjoy a pretend barbecue party together. Invite children to help you organise and cook the food. Set up a low square of bricks, leaving a gap in one side; balance a flat grill over this (a piece of strong slatted card will be fine) and have fun making a fire to go underneath, by crumpling up orange, yellow and red crêpe paper.

Let the children shape some food to be 'cooked', from play dough. They could make burgers, kebabs, bread rolls and fruit fritters. Use real tongs and fish slices to 'cook' the food over your fire. Demonstrate safety precautions as if you were having a real barbecue.

When your meal is ready, sit and pretend to eat together.

Music and movement
Play some rippling watery music while the children move around the room pretending to be fish. You could use recorded 'natural sounds', harp or classical guitar music which has a lilting quality or music from *The Blue Planet* soundtrack (George Fenton, BBC).

Suggest the children vary what sort of water creature they are: how would a shark swim? Or an octopus? What about a seahorse? Or a jellyfish?

Water play
Set out bowls of water in a safe outside area or indoors where spillages are not going to be a problem. Include some toy boats along with jugs, funnels, pumps and other water play toys. Provide a selection of items so that children can experiment to see what floats and what sinks: chat about what would make a good boat. Make sure the children have their sleeves well rolled up, are wearing aprons and are supervised at all times. Do not leave the water unattended.

Game time

5–10 mins

Magnetic fishing
You will need: silver card, black marker pen, metal paper clips, smooth bamboo cane, string, small magnets and a small paddling pool.

Make this game in advance. Cut out card fish, in sets of three, in various sizes. Enlarge the shape below and number each set: 1, 2, 3.

Fix some paper clips onto each fish. Make your fishing rods by attaching the cane and magnet to opposite ends of a length of string. (Keep the strings short to avoid accidents.) Set up the paddling pool and lay the fish in the bottom with the numbers showing. Younger children can simply play at catching fish. Others can catch their fish in order: 1, then 2, then 3.

Making time

15–30 mins

Under the sea
Use the 'Game time' fish shape and that on Activity page 37 to make plenty of fish shapes. Cut a variety of shapes and sizes from plain or coloured card, acetate, holographic or gift wrap paper. Work together to make a large poster or frieze of an underwater scene. Spread out a long strip of paper as a background: you will only want a few children working on this at any one time but give everyone an opportunity to contribute. Stick pieces of sandpaper along the bottom to make the seabed. Or mix sand, a little water and PVA glue to make a spreadable paste: the glue dries clear but holds the sand in place. Colourwash the rest of the background with runny blue paint.

Fish shapes can be decorated in all sorts of ways and added to the scene; seaweed strands can be cut from crêpe or tissue paper; more water can be shown with strips of blue tissue. See how varied and exciting your underwater scene can become!

Story time

10–15 mins

Breakfast with Jesus
It's difficult for young children to take individual roles but they will enjoy all being friends of Jesus with you. Remember that your voice and expression will set the atmosphere and draw the children into the events of the story.

Explain a little before you start about how fishing was done in Bible times: show a picture if you have one. It would be exciting to catch some fish but when they caught nothing, the fishermen would be tired, cold and disappointed.

Let's pretend to be friends of Jesus. We're feeling sad because Jesus seems to have gone away and we don't know when we'll see him again. We've decided to go fishing. So let's climb into our boat… and row it out to sea…

It's night time. Let's get hold of the nets and throw them over the edge of the boat into the water. Ready? Throw! Listen to the 'splash' as the nets hit the water… Now we have to wait a while… we have to sit quite still so the fish don't hear us and swim away.

It's time to see if we've caught any fish. We'll pull up the nets again. Are they heavy? Are they full of fish? Oh dear. We haven't caught any fish at all. Let's try again…

Still nothing?

Let's try again… *(Repeat several times but don't catch anything.)*

We've been fishing all night. It's almost morning now. We'd better go back to the shore. We haven't caught any fish. I'm tired, aren't you?

Just a moment! Look! Over there on the beach! There's a man waving to us. What's he saying? 'Have you caught any fish?' What shall we tell him? 'NO, WE HAVEN'T!'

What's he saying now? 'Try one more time.' But we've tried lots of times. We're not going to catch any fish now. Listen! He's still shouting. What's he saying? 'Put your nets out on the right-hand side of the boat. There will be some fish there!' Shall we try it? Which side is the 'right' side? Let's see what happens. Throw the nets out… what's this? The nets are getting heavy… so heavy we can't hold them… too heavy to pull into the boat… they are full of fish! Come on – we'll pull the nets to the shore and then we can get the fish out.

Let's row back to the shore… Do you know, I think I know who that man on the beach is. I think he's Jesus! Yes he is! And look! He's made a fire on the beach and he's got bread to eat. Jesus is saying, 'Bring some fish to cook for breakfast!' Come on, everyone. Let's go and have breakfast with Jesus!

Rhyme time

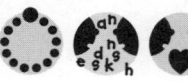

Fishing
Prepare to go fishing: will you catch anything? Yes!

Row, row, row. *(Sit on the floor and row.)*
Fish, fish, fish. *(Cast your fishing net, three times.)*
Wait, wait, wait. *(Sit and wait.)*
Fish! Fish! Fish! *(Shout!)*

I'm alive!
You can sing this rhyme if you wish to the traditional tune of 'Hot cross buns'.

I'm alive! I'm alive!
I can feel and jump and grow
'Cos I'm alive!

He's alive! He's alive!
Jesus died and rose again,
Now he's alive!

He's alive! He's alive!
Jesus cooked the bread and fish,
Now he's alive!

He's alive! He's alive!
Jesus said, 'I'll be with you,'
'Cos he's alive!

Song time

A man on the beach
Use this song to tell today's story. Explain that 'Galilee' was the area where the sea/big lake and the beach were. The tune is 'Row, row, row your boat'. Sing it a couple of times and then add actions as suggested by the words.

Sail, sail, sail your fishing boat
Out across the sea,
Wave, wave to the man
On the beach at Galilee.

Throw, throw, throw your nets
Throw them in the sea.
Pull, pull, pull them in,
Fish from Galilee.

Cook, cook, cook the fish
Caught freshly from the sea –
Breakfast time with Jesus
On the beach at Galilee.

Pray time

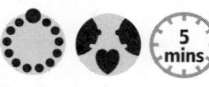

Catch a prayer
Use a large piece of netting (green plastic garden netting is ideal) to make a prayer net. Give each child a fish shape cut out of thin card or stiff paper. Ask them to think of something or someone they want to tell Jesus about. Help them write or draw their prayer on the fish. Spread the netting on the floor and let the children 'swim' their fish over to the netting and drop it in. When all the fish-prayers are caught, gather up the netting and hang it on the wall of your meeting room.

Extra time

•One, two, three, four, five, once I caught a fish alive' (traditional rhyme).

•Look at some reference books to see the amazing variety of fish.

•Organise an outing: this story links to various events or trips, perhaps a day at the beach, a pond-dipping expedition, a visit to an aquarium or a barbecue for all to enjoy. Invite other family members along and have a great time together!

Adults too

Think about the resurrection of Jesus and what it might mean for people today. The first followers of Jesus were convinced that he had come back to life. However, there have been many alternative theories to explain what happened: the authorities hid his body; Jesus' friends took the body; or Jesus only fainted on the cross and revived in the coolness of the tomb. Some say his resurrection was not literal. These and other possibilities are explored in the classic *Who Moved the Stone?* by Frank Morison (Faber), a lawyer who set out to prove the biblical accounts invalid.

The children in your group will have no difficulty in accepting the reality of a dead man returning to life, but the adults may be more sceptical. A belief in the resurrection of Jesus can mean a shift in everything our lives are built upon.

Further reading: *The Case for Christ*, Lee Strobel, Zondervan.

Top tip

Parents and full-time carers of a child with disabilities are the best people to give you advice and help on including their child. Do make time to talk to them: they know what their child's needs are and how best to meet those needs. If the usual carers do not stay at the group, the child may need a one-to-one helper. This will reassure parents that their child's needs will be met by one person with whom they can discuss issues and develop a trusting relationship.

ACTIVITY PAGE:
The photocopiable activity page for this outline is on page 37

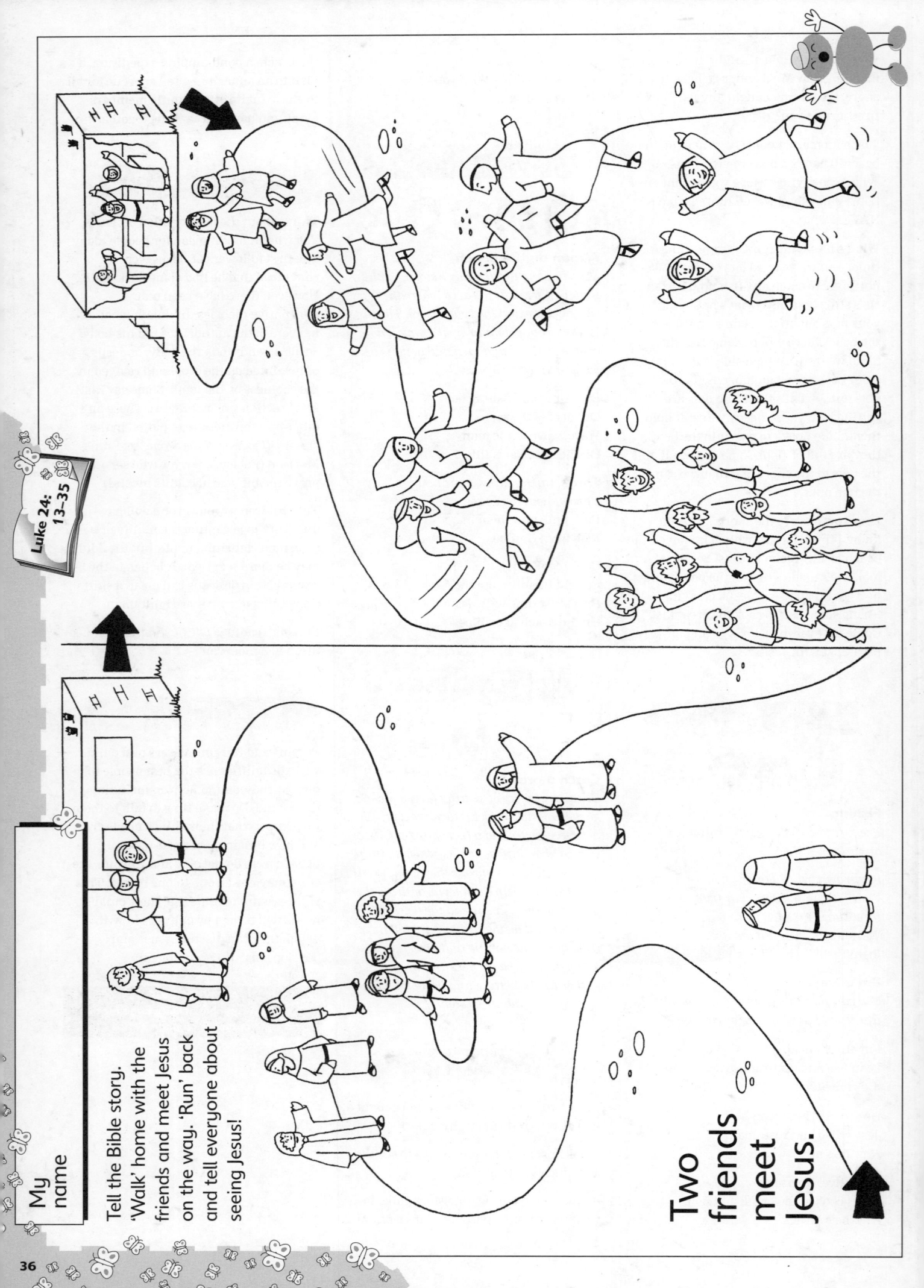

My name

What will your fish look like? Colour the fish, cover it in shiny foil shapes or make fingerprint patterns all over it.

John 21: 1–14

Jesus and his friends cooked fish for breakfast.

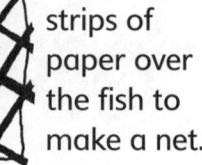

Catch some fish. 
Make some fish.  Stick them on a big piece of paper. 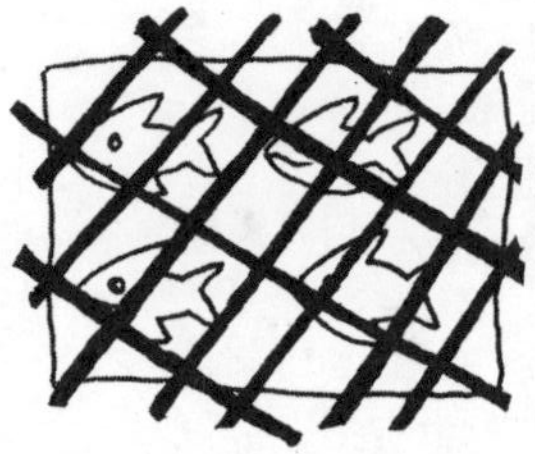 Criss-cross strips of paper over the fish to make a net.

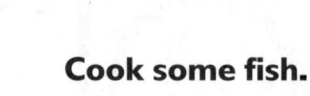

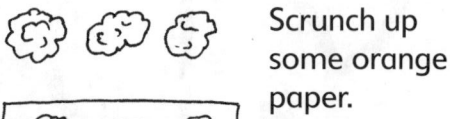

Cook some fish.
Scrunch up some orange paper.  Stick it on a piece of stiff card. Make some fish. Put them on top of your 'fire' to cook!

37

9 Easter
Jesus goes to heaven

Luke 24: 50–53; Acts 1:9–11

Play time

Look up

If you can do so safely and easily, go outside and look at the clouds together (or look through a window). Ask the children to spot different shapes and types of clouds and watch them as they move across the sky or hang stationary. Encourage the children to observe the sky: is it just one colour? Is it blue? Is it covered with cloud or is there no cloud at all? (Remind them not to look directly at the sun.) Alternatively, show pictures of clouds in books about the weather.

Paint some large-scale pictures of the clouds and the sky or use cotton wool and glue fluffy clouds on a painted sky background. This could be done all together or individually.

So long, farewell

Think of all the words and ways you know of saying goodbye. Make a list of them all: include 'baby talk' (ta-ta) and other languages (encourage the adults to join in and help with this); and non-verbal ways – blow a kiss, wave hands. Adapt the 'Mulberry bush' game to practise all the ways you've thought of: this is the way we wave goodbye; this is how we say *'au revoir'*; this is the way we bow 'namaste'.

Balloons, bubbles and bouncing balls

Clear plenty of space and let the children play freely with one of these options.

Try it out

You will need: a discovery area with natural objects on display. Include a stone, stick, shell, feather, leaf, flower.

Gather a couple of children around at a time. What will happen with each of these items if you drop it? Choose one and test it out. Repeat with other items. All fall to the ground. Nothing floats up. But when God took Jesus to heaven, he went up into the sky!

Game time

Travelling on

Play a miming game, with some of your toy vehicles as examples. Get in a plane to fly to America. Jump in a rocket to go to the moon. Clatter along in a steam train. Rumble along in a bus to the shops. Mention that Jesus went to heaven, but he didn't travel on any of the vehicles you've played with: God had a special and amazing way of taking him to heaven. If you are going to tell the story later, remind the children to listen out carefully to find how Jesus travelled. If you are not using the story, simply say that God took him to heaven in a cloud.

Floating clouds

All lie on the floor with eyes closed and ask the children to do the following. Imagine you are a cloud up in the sky… you're floating… floating… floating along… Use a gentle, lilting voice to describe how they might be feeling with the soft air all around them and the light wind blowing. Watch the children as you play this and stop when they start to get restless.

Making time

Heaven mobile

You will need: three chenille wires, four varying lengths of cotton, a cloud, sun, moon and star per child, PVA glue, a couple of shallow trays containing different coloured glitter, a hole punch.

Make a hole in the cloud, sun, moon and star. Give them to the children, to cover with glue and then dip into the glitter. Leave to dry. Demonstrate how to make the mobile. Bend each end of two wires making a closed loop at each end. Twist the wires around each other to make a cross. Tie a length of thread onto each loop. Twist one end of the third wire round the crossover, shaping the other end to form a hanging hook.

When the glittery shapes are dry, tie them onto the thread to complete the mobile.

Display them hanging as high up in the room as you can so you can look up and see them.

Story time

Jesus goes to heaven

Tell the story using balloon characters.

You will need: a coloured balloon for each child, two white balloons (angels) and a helium-filled balloon (Jesus), all inflated and with string attached, adhesive stickers, a helper to introduce the angels during the story.

Show the children how they can put the stickers on their balloons to make faces. Say that their balloons are going to be the 'friends of Jesus' in your story. You may be able to go outside to tell the story but make sure you have tied the string loosely to each child's wrist or a buttonhole. Don't release the balloons on purpose: it may upset the children to lose them and is also a pollution hazard.

It was time for Jesus to go to heaven.

Jesus and his friends went for a walk up a hill. *(Invite the children to bring their balloon characters with them and walk round the room or on the spot.)* When they got to the top of the hill, Jesus spoke to his friends. 'Tell everyone about me,' he said. 'Everywhere you go, tell people about me.' Then he promised them that one day soon, he would send his Holy Spirit to help them. It was time for Jesus to go to heaven to be with his Father God.

Jesus said goodbye to his friends. *(Let your Jesus-balloon say goodbye to all the others.)*

They looked. And watched. And they saw Jesus go up into the sky. *(Loosen but don't fully let go of your string.)* Not by plane or rocket or helicopter. Not even by balloon. God took him into the sky and he was hidden by the clouds.

(Have an assistant produce the two white balloons and say that two men dressed in white suddenly appeared.) They were angels. They asked Jesus' friends, 'Why are you all looking up into the sky?' *(Let the balloon-angels explain that Jesus has gone back to heaven and that one day he will come back the same way.)* Now, the friends of Jesus are to do the important job that Jesus asked them to do: tell everyone about Jesus! *(While the children are distracted by the angels, hide the Jesus-balloon from sight so that he has 'disappeared' when they look again.)*

Say that the friends of Jesus did tell other people about him – and they told other people – and that's how we can know about Jesus today.

Rhyme time

4 mins

Up to heaven
This rhyme also goes to the tune of 'Incy wincy spider'.

Jesus went to heaven,
Hidden in the clouds.
His friends were watching,
And they said out loud,
'We'll do as Jesus asked us
Tell everyone we know,
That Jesus is the greatest friend
That anyone can know.'

Into the sky
Pretend to watch Jesus go to heaven with this action chant:

Up, up, up, *(Crouch down and slowly come up.)* x 4
High, high, high, *(Raise arms high in the air.)* x 4
Jesus goes… *(Reach up high, standing on tiptoe.)* x 4
Into the sky. *(Look up.)* x 4

Song time

3 mins

Good news!
Jesus asked his friends to tell everyone about him: this song gives us the opportunity to do that. And the best news is that Jesus loves us all!

Sing to the tune of 'Ho, ho, ho hosanna' (KS 109) and vary the volume of singing on each verse: normal, quiet, loud.

I have some news to tell you,
I have some news to tell you,
I have some news to tell you,
Jesus loves us all!

I have some news to whisper, . . .
Jesus loves us all!

I have some news to shout about, . . .
Jesus loves us all!

Think more about going away with traditional singing rhymes like: 'The bear went over the mountain'; 'Five little ducks' and 'The wheels on the bus'.

Pray time

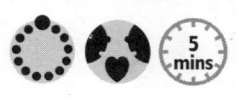

5 mins

Where is heaven?
Chat about what the children think heaven will be like; everyone has different ideas. The Bible gives us some word pictures. Read a few verses of Revelation, and pick out phrases that you think the children will enjoy from 21:10 – 22:5. We can be sure that heaven will be wonderful and that Jesus will be there to take care of us.

Repeat or play the game 'Floating clouds' from Game time. This time, while the children are lying quietly with their eyes closed, ask them to imagine how lovely it is in heaven with Jesus. Use words from Revelation again to set the scene and describe Jesus being there. Sing quietly 'Jesus, Jesus here I am', JU p96.

Extra time

- Sing the action songs 'If you climb', *JU* p12 and 'Wide, wide as the ocean', p72.
- Play the dancing game 'Holy hokey', *JU* p22.
- Read the story aloud from *The Lion Storyteller Bible*, Bob Hartman.

Adults too

The angels' task was to explain things to the friends of Jesus. 'Jesus hasn't just gone into the sky – he's gone to heaven.' But that doesn't help us much! No one knows where or exactly what these heavenly realms are – and we can feel as baffled and overawed as that little group of early followers on the hilltop. Paul assures those who believe in Jesus that they will be with Jesus for ever 'in the future world' (Ephesians 2:7–10).

You may know the Korean parable which explains the difference between heaven and hell. In both places, people sit round a table spread with a wonderful banquet which they have to eat with 2 metre long chopsticks. In hell, everyone is miserable because they can't get the food to their mouths without it dropping from the chopsticks; in heaven, the party is steaming ahead because the people have learned to feed one another.

Top tip

What's Heaven Like? Stephanie King, God and Me Books, SU.

'Will I need a bath in heaven? Will heaven be fun? Will there be parties in heaven?' Have you ever struggled to answer young children's questions, in terms they understand? This little book will help you. Using simple pictures and brief text, it is ideal for sharing this concept with young children.

ACTIVITY PAGE:
The photocopiable activity page for this outline is on page 42

10 Easter
Pentecost

Acts 2

Play time

Can you see it?
Some play and talkabout ideas to help the children understand that some things are real even though they cannot be seen. Link this to the fact that God can't be seen.

Blow – hold your hands up a little way from your face and blow gently. What can you feel? Watch each other do this. Can you see anything coming out of your mouths? We can feel the air but we can't see it.

Wind – look out of the window. Is it a windy day? How do you know from what you can see? Imagine it is very windy and try to walk across the room. What happens? Does your hair blow or your hat come off? Are you cold? Are the leaves blowing on the trees? Can we see the wind blowing? We can see what it does but we can't see the wind itself.

Bubbles – mix up about two litres of bubble mix and pour it into large bowls, so several children can play at once. Set the bowls on a firm surface and provide plenty of bubble sticks or show children how to touch index finger and thumb together to make a circle, dip your hand into the liquid and then blow bubbles from the film across your hand. Blow, chase and catch bubbles. What happens when the bubble pops? What do they feel on their skin? The bubble has gone but there is some wetness which we can feel.

Big play – let children play on stable swings and trampolines (with adult supervision). Can they feel the air touching them as they swoop or bounce?

As you play together, take any opportunity to comment that we can't see God but we know he is there, because of everything he does.

Game time

Is it really there?
You will need: a tambourine, a shaker and some bells.

Put the instruments in front of you and demonstrate each one. Ask the children to do a different action each time they hear the sound. Try these out a few times. Then take the instruments behind a screen and play each one. As you play, mention that the children can still know what to do even though they can't see the instruments any more. How do they know? Because they can still hear the sound and that tells them.

Jesus loves you
Prepare a box with an unbreakable mirror fixed in the bottom. Tell the children you have a special picture and you're going to show it to them one at a time. Let each child in turn look into the box and say to them, 'This is someone who Jesus loves very much.' Make sure they realise it's them who Jesus loves!

Making time

Aflame!
Cut a strip of card long enough to go round a child's head. Allow the child to decorate the band, with adhesive shapes or crayons. Cut out flame shapes in different colours and sizes. Stick several of these together to form a multi-coloured flame. Fix the flame to the centre of the band. Measure the strip so that it fits the individual child, cut off the excess card, and tape together to form a circle.

Like a dove
Make the dove models from Activity page 43. Mention that the dove is sometimes used to remind us of God's Holy Spirit. If you hang the doves from thin shirring elastic, they will bounce up and down as the children hold them.

Story time

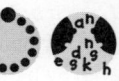

God sends the Holy Spirit
Explain that sometimes people who are special to us have to go away from us. We know they still remember us because they send us letters and cards or speak to us on the phone. Jesus had to go away and leave his friends but he had a way of helping them, even when they couldn't see him.

Jesus' friends were very sad and afraid. Jesus had gone away. He had said goodbye to them and gone to be with God in heaven. Jesus had promised to send them someone to help them. But they didn't know who it would be or when they would come.

All the friends of Jesus were together in a big room, upstairs in a house. They had been talking about Jesus and the promise of special help Jesus had made to them. 'What did Jesus mean?' they wondered.

Suddenly all the people in the room heard a loud noise. It sounded just like a strong gust of wind. The windy noise swept through the house, up the stairs and blew open the door of the room where they were sitting.

The wind became stronger. The friends of Jesus began to feel stronger too. They felt warm inside and braver and braver. Little lights appeared above their heads, like tiny flames. They smiled and hugged each other. Jesus had sent his Holy Spirit to them. Everything was going to be all right! Jesus was still with them, even though they couldn't see him. He was still their special friend. They wanted to shout and dance. They were laughing and clapping and dancing for joy and singing happy songs to God.

A big crowd of people had gathered outside the house. They wondered what was going on. Peter looked out of the window and saw all the people standing there. 'I'm going to tell everyone about Jesus,' he said. So Peter ran down the stairs and outside. He stood in front of the big crowd of people and he told them how much Jesus loved them – and that they could be friends of Jesus too.

Peter and his friends told everyone about Jesus. They were not scared or worried any more. Something wonderful had happened to them, making them brave and very, very happy. God had sent his Holy Spirit to be with them and help them, just as Jesus had promised.

Rhyme time

On the day of Pentecost
A retelling of the Bible story. Use verses 1–3 to make a shorter rhyme.

Friends of Jesus met together
In a room where they could pray.
They said, 'Jesus, how we love you,
Though we can't see you today.'

Friends of Jesus, quietly waiting,
Heard a noise like rushing air,
Saw what looked like flames of fire
Rest on everybody there.

Friends of Jesus, all together,
Thanked God for his power and love.
Went outside where crowds of people
Heard them praising God above!

Friends of Jesus – up spoke Peter,
Told the crowd, 'You ought to know –
God sent you his own son, Jesus!
Be his friends too! Don't be slow!'

Friends of Jesus, many people
Joined God's family that day.
Learned just how much Jesus loved them,
Learned to trust him and obey.

Friends of Jesus, there are millions
Who have joined God's family.
Let's be glad that our friend, Jesus
Loves them all, including me!

Song time

Receive
This song, to the tune of 'All things bright and beautiful', affirms our relationship with Jesus who can be real to us even though we cannot see him.

We may not see you Jesus, but –
We know that you are near,
And when we sing and talk to you,
We know you always hear.

You sent the Holy Spirit,
To make your promise clear,
That when we sing and talk to you,
We know you always hear.

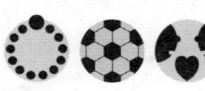

We may not see you Jesus, but –
We know that you are near,
And when we sing and talk to you,
We know you always hear.

Pray time

Then and now
The two verses of this action prayer compare and contrast the experience of the early church and our experience today: Jesus sends his Holy Spirit to be with all of us.

Repeat the same actions in the second verse.

Jesus' friends were lonely and afraid.
(Curl up.)
Jesus' friends were waiting for his help.
(Look around.)
Jesus sent his friends the Holy Spirit,
(Begin to stand up.)
To make them strong and brave and happy in his love.
(Stretch arms up high.)

Sometimes I am lonely and afraid.
Sometimes I am waiting for your help.
Thank you that you sent the Holy Spirit,
To make me strong and brave and happy in your love.

Extra time

- Sing 'Jesus' love is very wonderful', *JU* p14.
- Make a fan. Fold stiff paper in a concertina. Tape one end together and open out the folds to make a fan: feel the wind as you wave and flap.
- 'The Holy Spirit' p73 and 'At Pentecost', p75, *LACH*.
- 'Just as Jesus said', *LSS*, p69.

The windy day, a Teddy Horsley book, NCEC, explores how we can experience things we cannot see.

Adults too

Trying to explain the work of the Holy Spirit in our lives is not always easy; it's a personal thing and can be difficult to put into words. It's also a very public thing and people may be sceptical or worried, having heard or seen media coverage of remarkable practices and events. Be ready to discuss what goes on in your church or fellowship and give reassurance if necessary. This definition may help you; it's from Corrie ten Boom, author of *The Hiding Place*, and concentration camp survivor, who said:

'I have a glove here in my hand. The glove cannot do anything by itself, but, when my hand is in it, it can do many things. True, it is not the glove, but my hand in the glove that acts.

We are gloves. It is the Holy Spirit in us who is the hand, who does the job. We have to make room for the hand so that every finger is filled.'

Top tip

Toy libraries are an excellent resource for your group. You will be able to borrow a wide range of equipment. Some libraries make a small charge, some only charge for large items. To find out if you have a toy library in your area ask at your community centre, or contact your local government offices.

ACTIVITY PAGE:
The photocopiable activity page for this outline is on page 43

Copy the page directly onto white card, if possible.

Luke 24: 50-53; Acts 1:9-11

Make a flag.

Turn this page into a flag. Decorate both sides as brightly as you can. Wrap this edge around a handle (a garden cane, dowel, stiff artstraw) and hold in place with sticky tape. Wave your flag and think about Jesus going to heaven.

My name

42

My name

Acts 2

Cut out the dove body from white card. Make the slit as shown. Pleat a rectangle of white paper. Push it through the slit. Fan out to make wings. You could make lots of doves and hang them from a wire coat hanger to make a mobile.

43

11 God gives us families
Mothers
Sarah

Genesis 18:1–15; 21:1–8

Play time

Food for fun
You will need: play dough in green, yellow and red, baking tins, cutters, rolling pins and boards, a sheet.

Erect a 'play tent' or make a tent from chairs and a sheet. Have some small tables and chairs. Talk to the children about what happens when visitors come to their house – what do the grown-ups do, eg ask them to sit down, give them a drink or something to eat? Encourage the children to 'play' those things and to 'make' the food that might be prepared for their meal from play dough. Provide each child with a plastic 'play' plate or a small paper plate so that they can put their 'food' onto it.

Bread
Let a few children at a time, work with real bread dough. Quick-mix packet bread dough from supermarkets is ideal. Make it up beforehand so that it is ready to be moulded. Give each child a piece of dough to make it into a shape then place each roll onto a baking tray. Draw a plan of the rolls on the tray, with names, so that there is no confusion later! Bake in the oven then give out to the children when cool. As with any activity involving food, hygiene and safety are important. Check on food allergies, particularly gluten. For safety, have one adult responsible for the cooking and keep children away from the hot area.

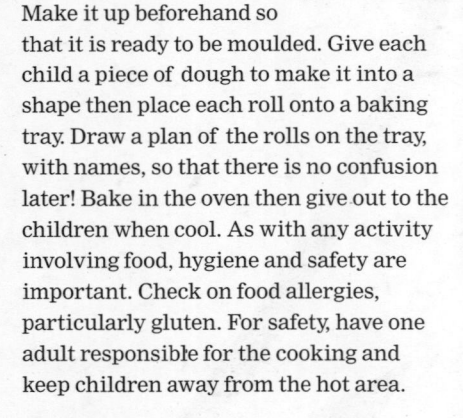

Away from home
To engage the children in the idea of parents working outside the home, set up an 'office' corner with a table and chair, pad of paper, pencils, toy phone and calculator. Set out other toys for free play which relate to non-home working, eg farming, driving, shop or factory work.

They could also be encouraged to draw a picture of 'what Mummy does during the day'.

Game time

Mummy says…
Have the children standing in a space big enough for them to move around a little. Explain that when you shout out an instruction to them, they have to do it if it is preceded by 'Mummy says'. An example would be 'Mummy says, sit on the floor'. They all have to sit on the floor. If you shout 'Sit on the floor' they should remain where they are. Vary the instructions so that some involve more physical exercise, eg, 'Mummy says, run around the room' and some more precise movement: 'Mummy says, brush your teeth.'

Add variety by inviting any mothers present to lead the game!

This game needs a lot of concentration but play it for fun: no one need be penalised for making a mistake.

Making time

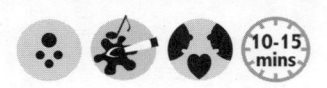

I love my mum
You will need: A4 card, glue sticks, yellow circles of card or paper for petals, brown circles for the centres, stems and leaves from green card, plant pot shape from holographic card.

Make a card for the children to give to their mother (or carer, see Top tip). Have all the pieces cut out ready so children can assemble the card.

Fold a piece of A4 card. Have glue sticks available so that the children can create a flower picture from the materials available on the front.

Inside the card, tape a sunflower seed then let the children stick on a photocopy of these words:

Plant this seed
And watch it grow.
As it grows tall
I'll be growing taller too.

Underneath stick on a red heart with 'Mummy' or the name of another carer written in the middle. Photocopy these words for each child to stick under the heart:

'Thank you for looking after me.
I love you and God does too.'

Let the children 'sign' the cards themselves.

Story time

Sarah is a mum
Have a glove puppet on your hand (Johnny). Get him to communicate in your ear and then tell the children what he has said. You'll also need a Russian stacking doll with just the smallest one inside; and three simple stick puppets to represent the visitors.

We're going to say thank you for our mummies today. What do our mummies do for us? Can you think of anything, Johnny? *(Rubs hands across his face.)* Johnny says his mummy washes his face. Can anyone else think of anything? *(Pause for the children to suggest things. End up with the puppet putting his arms across himself and whispering.)* Johnny's mummy gives him hugs.

(Show the children a Russian doll.) This is a woman called Sarah. She loved God, but she was sad because she hadn't any children. She would like to be a mummy and give hugs and *(include the list of things that the children shouted out)*. She thinks she is too old to be a mummy now.

One day three men *(three circles with faces, stuck on flat craft sticks)* passed the tent where Sarah lived. Abraham, her husband, wanted to look after them. He asked them to stay for dinner. Sarah went inside the tent and started to cook and bake. Soon a lovely dinner was ready. What would you like for your dinner? They ate some meat and some lovely fresh bread and drank some milk.

Sarah did the clearing up in the tent. She could hear the men talking outside. Suddenly she had a big surprise! She heard one of the men say, 'Sarah is going to have a baby!' Next year Sarah would be a mummy! Sarah thought they were joking. She laughed and laughed and laughed. Can you laugh loudly?

'I'm too old,' she said, 'I can't have a baby.' The men said that it was not a joke. God was going to make her a mummy. God had promised Sarah would have her own baby to look after.

And do you know what? Next year Sarah had a baby boy. *(Open Russian doll to find the smallest one inside.)* She called him Isaac. She loved him very much. I think she carried on laughing because she was so happy.

Chat about how names often have meanings. Isaac's name means 'laughter'

Rhyme time

Sarah's baby

Allow plenty of time for children to work out what to do with their fingers as you lead this finger rhyme. Exaggerate your actions to make it easier for them to copy.

One woman, Sarah, standing in her tent, *(Hold one index finger up.)*
Sarah and Abraham, old and nearly bent, *(Hold up both index fingers.)*
Three men travelling, come to tell them news, *(Hold up three fingers on one hand.)*
Five people eat the bread that Sarah had, *(Hold up one hand.)*
Three tell the other two about a baby son. *(Hold up little finger on other hand.)*
One woman, Sarah, in her tent today, *(Touch index fingers together to form a triangle shape.)*
God's given her a baby, she laughs and laughs – hooray! *(Lace fingers together, palms upwards and rock, as a cradle.)*

Song time

Sarah laughs

Start with everyone standing in a circle. At the end of each line, clap twice; on the fourth line, turn round on the spot. Sing to the tune of 'Here we go Looby Lou'.

This is how Sarah laughed, (Ha, ha!)
This is how Sarah laughed, (Ha, ha!)
This is how Sarah laughed, (Ha, ha!)
When three men gave her the good news!

Isaac's the baby God gave, (Hooray!) . . .
God promised and gave Sarah a son!

Now Sarah's a mummy at last, ...
She's glad to take care of her child!

Pray time

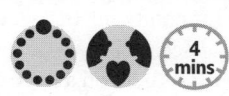

Thank you, God

Before the session collect a small twiggy branch from a tree and put it in a pot filled with soil so that it looks like a miniature tree. Prepare a cardboard female figure for each child. Punch a hole in the top and thread through a loop of wool.

During the session give each child a figure. Put the crayons out and encourage them to draw their mum (or another carer). Then place the 'tree' in the centre of the circle of children. Each child will take it in turns to loop their 'Mum' on the tree and everyone will say together 'Dear God, thank you for … (name of child)'s mummy.'

My family

I love them and they love me,
Thank you for my family.

When we're sad and need your care,
Thank you, God, that you are there.

I love them…

When we argue and we fight,
Help us, God, to make things right.

I love them…

Extra time

- Make a photo frame as a gift. Use a piece of stiff A5 card with a 2.5 cm frame stuck on top (glue along three sides so that the photograph can slip in); decorate with painted thumb prints.

- *My Mum is Fantastic* and *My Grandma is Wonderful,* Nick Butterworth, Walker Books.

- Role play what mums do at home; remember they're allowed to play as well as work!

- Play with a Russian stacking doll toy.

Adults too

How sad it must have been for Sarah, as it is for other women in her position, to go through disappointment month after month. It must have seemed as though it was possible for every other woman in the world to enter into motherhood except Sarah. In the culture of the time, a large family was a sign of God's blessing. If you had no children, people thought it must be because God was displeased with you, so Sarah's lack of children was a spiritual as well as a physical and emotional burden.

For those of us with children let's be constantly thankful for them (even if they keep us awake all night!) and remember that they are a gift from God.

Top tip

This session would be an ideal one to use in preparation for Mothering Sunday. Most families, whether they are 'religious' or not enjoy marking this festival and will be delighted with their children's efforts at card-making.

It is important to be sensitive to any children who are not cared for by their mother and to find out who their particular 'carer' is so that the craft can be directed to that person and other activities adapted accordingly.

ACTIVITY PAGE:
The photocopiable activity page for this outline is on page 48

12 God gives us families
Fathers
Jacob gives Joseph a coat

Genesis 37:1–11

Play time

Dough daddies
While the children are at the dough table, suggest they mould and shape a figure to represent their dad (or grandad, uncle or other male family member). Provide shaped cutters if available but also encourage the children to shape their figures using their hands only.

Be a dad
Make sure your home corner contains plenty of equipment that a father might use. Chat to the children while they play about their fathers and the sort of things their dads are good at. Are all dads good at the same things?

Book corner
Create a cosy book area, with rugs on the floor, giant cushions and bean bags. Provide books with family themes, particularly fathers, like the modern classics *Guess How Much I Love You*, (Sam McBratney, Walker Books) and *Peace at Last,* (Jill Murphy, Picturemac.) Other books which give a positive message include *My Dad is Brilliant* and *My Grandpa is Amazing*, (Nick Butterworth, Walker Books) and *Daddy's Lullaby*, (Tony Bradman, Bloomsbury.) Try to have an adult helper in the book corner who can talk to the children about the books, read sections or whole books to them and chat about the stories and themes.

Put on your coat
Help children learn to put on their coats by themselves. Follow these simple steps. Each child needs plenty of space around them.

1 Kneel or crouch on the floor. 2 Spread your coat in front of you with the collar near your knees and the outer side of the coat downwards. 3 Push both your hands into the sleeves. 4 Start to stand up and as you do so, push your arms further into the sleeves, and lift the coat over your head, so it hangs down your back. You're now wearing your coat!

Game time

Dance to your daddy
To play this dancing game, form two lines facing each other, about 2 m apart, girls in one and boys in the other. Boys dance the first verse, while girls sing; then swap over. Plenty of adult involvement will help this go well.

Dance to your daddy, my little laddies,
(Hold hands along the row, skip three steps forward.)
Dance to your daddy, my little lads.
(Three steps back.)
You shall have a fishy, on a little dishy,
(Clap.)
You shall have a fishy when the boat comes in. *(Turn on the spot.)*
Dance to your daddy, my little laddies,
Dance to your daddy, my little lads.

Dance to your daddy, my little lasses,
Dance to your daddy, my little lass.
You shall have a fishy, on a little dishy,
You shall have a fishy when the boat comes in.
Dance to your daddy, my little lasses,
Dance to your daddy, my little lass.

Making time

My dad

You will need: paper, card, paint, pasta, PVA glue.

Paint or draw a picture of 'My dad' or another adult carer. When dry, mount this on a large piece of stiff card, leaving a generous margin round the edge.

Take another piece of card the same size and cut out a hole in the centre to make a frame. Glue pieces of pasta around this and when dry, paint with a metallic or bright paint. Lay this on top of the picture and glue into place.

Great dad!
Make 'great dad' cards – any day can be 'father's day'. Fold a thick piece of paper or card in half and draw a person-shape on the front, as shown. Cut out, then add clothes and features. Let the child 'write' a message inside to say that Dad is great!

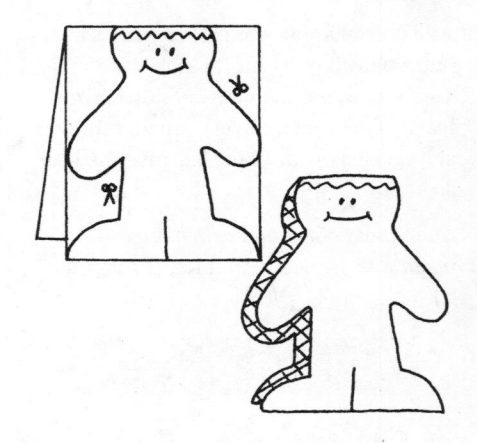

Story time

A coat for Joseph
A children's Bible will have pictures to illustrate this story.

How many children are there in your family? One? Four? Has anyone here got twelve brothers and sisters? There is a family in the Bible where there were thirteen children: twelve sons and one daughter. The father of this family was a man called Jacob.

Jacob was a farmer. He was a very good farmer. He had many sheep and many goats. As Jacob's sons grew up, they learned to look after the animals and to be good farmers too.

Jacob had a big family, but they were not always a very happy family. Jacob's twelve sons were not all good friends. You see, Jacob loved all his children. But he loved one of them more than the others. One of his youngest sons was called Joseph and Jacob loved Joseph best of all. This made the other sons unhappy.

One day, when Joseph was seventeen, Jacob gave him a coat. It was a beautiful coat. It was made of lovely patterned and coloured cloth. It was a long coat with long sleeves. And it was the sort of coat that is only worn by someone very important. Joseph was very pleased to have such a beautiful coat to wear. The coat meant that Joseph was more important than any of his brothers. The coat meant that his father, Jacob, loved Joseph very much.

(If you want a shorter story, finish here.)

What do you think Joseph's brothers thought when they saw the beautiful coat? They were cross! They didn't want to be friends with Joseph any more.

Joseph was a bit of a show-off. He was always having dreams and in his dreams, he was always very important. One morning he said, 'Guess what I dreamed last night? I dreamed the sun, the moon and the stars bowed down to me!'

His brothers just thought he was showing off again. But his father, Jacob, thought about the dream.

'Do you mean,' he asked, 'that we are all going to bow to you, like bowing to the king? Me, your mother and your brothers, like the sun, the moon and the stars in your dream?'

Jacob did not think a dream like that could ever come true. But he did wonder about it and about his young son Joseph.

Look in a children's Bible to see how the dream did come true, after many adventures for Jacob and his family along the way.

Rhyme time

Two busy fathers

A finger rhyme. Use one finger from each hand to be the fathers in this rhyme. Or mime some actions to the words. Shout out the very last line!

Two busy fathers walking down the street,
One named David, one named Pete.
To the office, David. To the factory, Pete.
Come home David. Come home Pete.

Fathers with their children
　going to the park,
One named Stephen, one named Mark.
To the playground, Stephen.
　To the duckpond Mark.
Home time, Stephen. Home time, Mark.

Two sleepy fathers early in the day.
One named Wesley, one named Ray.
Read the paper, Wesley. Feed the baby, Ray.
WAKE UP, WESLEY! WAKE UP, RAY!

Song time

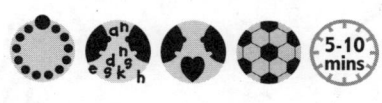

Thank you for my family

This song goes to the tune of 'Stand up, clap hands' (JP 225).

Stand up, clap hands,
　shout, 'Thank you, Lord,
For people who look after me!'
Stand up, clap hands,
　shout, 'Thank you, Lord,
I'm part of your family.'

When I look around
　at the people who care,
For me and my friends,
　I'm glad we can share,
The wonderful world God's given to us –
I'm glad to be part of God's family!
Stand up…

Pray time

Best dad

You will need: adults to act as scribes.

This prayer is by five-year-old Meg.

> Thank you, God, for my dad.
> He makes me smile.
> He holds my hand.
> He gives me big hugs.
> He mends my toys.
> I love him.

Encourage the children to make up their own prayers about their dads or others who care for them at home. Note down what the children are saying. Ask the children to paint or draw pictures of the person they have made the prayer about. While they are doing this, write out their words neatly and clearly. Mount the pictures and the prayers on coloured backing paper.

Give each child their own prayer picture to hold and to look at quietly for a few moments.

Extra time

- Look in a nature encyclopedia to find some amazing animal fathers: emperor penguins carry their chicks on their feet, ostriches look after large broods and seahorses carry their babies in a pouch.

Adults too

Have you any male carers with the group today? Think about how you can make them welcome without making them cringe! (Don't use them as a visual aid for this topic!)

Jesus referred to God as his 'father' and encouraged his followers to speak to God as 'Our Father'. For many people the concept of the fatherhood of God is a positive and secure one but for some, the imagery is less helpful. For those with memories of little or poor fathering or of an abusive father-figure, 'God the Father' is not a comforting person. This topic may well stir up mixed reactions: be prepared to spend time with those who may be hurting. Make sure you know of Christian counselling services available for adults – and possibly for children too.

Top tip

For many children and families, it's fun to think about dads and to thank God for them. But, for other families it may be more difficult. If there are children in your group with no dad, some of these activities will need to be adapted to suit someone else, male or female, who is well known to the child. If necessary, miss out activities. This is where knowing your group well will be particularly important, so that you don't cause offence, distress or confusion. Above all be sensitive.

ACTIVITY PAGE:
The photocopiable activity page for this outline is on page 49

Genesis 18:1–15; 21:1–8

My name

Sarah was very happy when she had a baby boy.

Here is Sarah. Cut out the picture of baby Isaac for Sarah to hold.

Stick the picture of Isaac in place.

Or

If you link Isaac and Sarah with a paper fastener, you can help Sarah rock her baby to sleep.

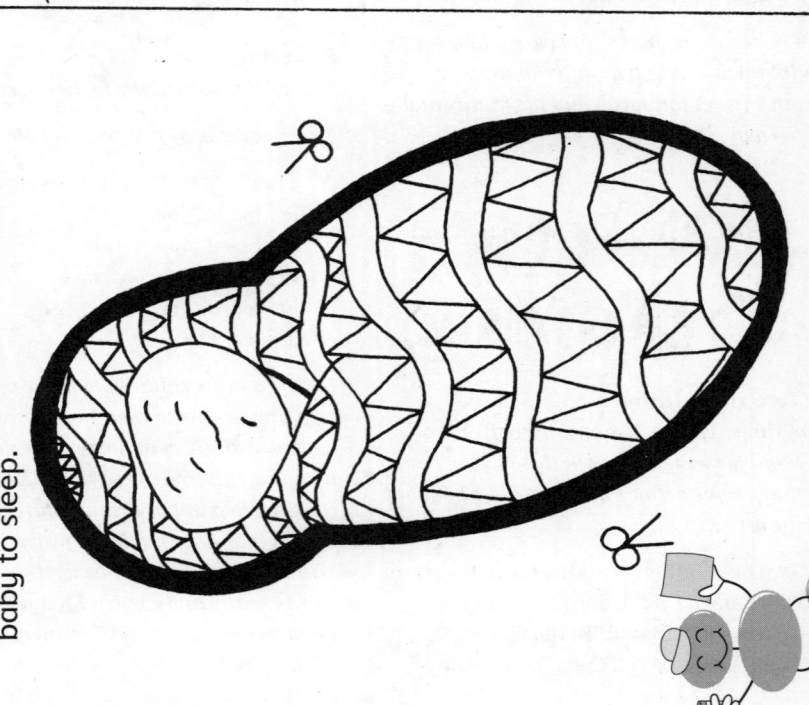

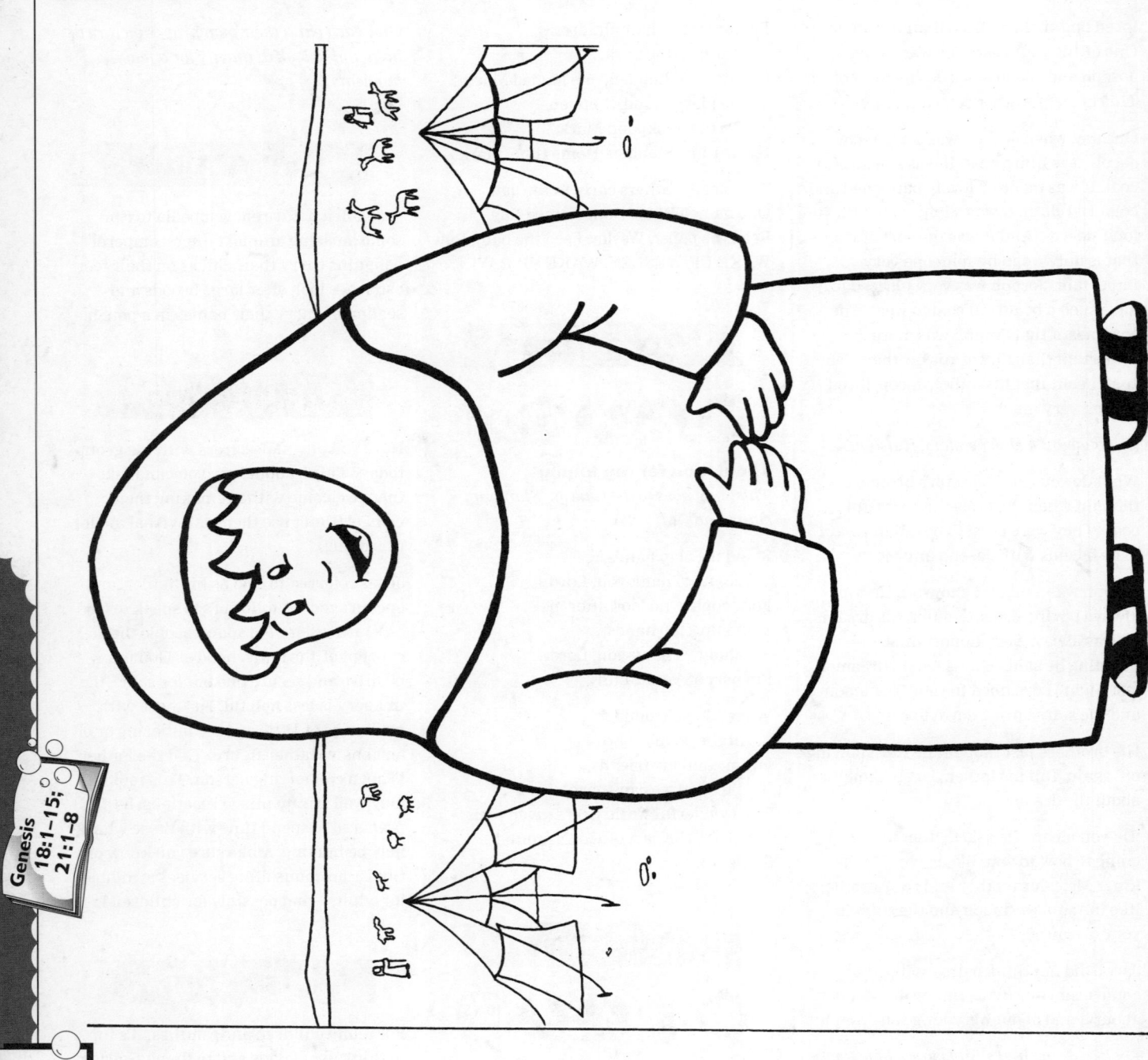

48

My name

Genesis 37: 1-11

Jacob was father to twelve sons and one daughter.
He gave his son Joseph a lovely coat.

Count the children in father Jacob's big family.

49

13 God gives us families
Brothers
Jacob and Esau

Genesis 25: 19–34; 27;33

Play time

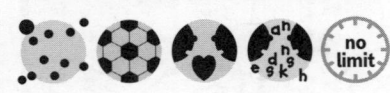

You will need: large outdoor toys, doll's house, dolls and furniture, construction toys, eg Duplo, home corner or play house, dressing up clothes, sand tray, blocks.

Big play
If some of the play time can be outside, this will give the children an experience of Esau's joy at being outside as well as the more normal inside play. If you have a seesaw and slide these could be taken outside as long as a safe landing surface is provided. Large beach balls are soft and fun for small hands. A few ride-on toys would be useful to give variety. If space or equipment outside are limited it is better to take small groups for a shorter time rather than risk disputes over who will ride the tricycle. Also keeping children safe is easier with only a few children. Depending on your circumstances you may feel it necessary for parents and carers to come out with their children.

Small-scale play
Indoors, set up all the toys you can which encourage imaginative play, have a family of dolls for the doll's house, with all the things they need. (If you do not have a doll's house a simple one can be made from four shoeboxes stuck together and with wallpaper or sticky-backed plastic inside. Set out the equipment needed to make a Duplo house, and have sets of animals or people to live in it. Have a tea table set out in the play house.

Setting the scene
Provide a sand tray with wooden blocks, or miniature houses. Encourage the children to build a town and talk about who lives there. Are there brothers and sisters in the houses?

Game time

Matching games
There are many simple matching games available or you can make your own. Try to have a variety of simple, one to one matching and also one to several, eg shoes per person. As the children match the sets talk about what they are doing and why they are making their choices. Variations on pairs and lotto games can be purchased from educational toy stockists.

Happy families
For younger children this can be an extension of the matching game above. Older children may be able to play a simplified version of the game. Give each child three cards. Spread the rest out on the table in front of them. Now let each child in turn take or swap a card until they have a whole family. Use the game as an opportunity to reinforce the counting of numbers up to four.

Making time

Two brothers
You will need: circles of card or paper plates, crayons, a selection of smooth shiny fabrics and fluffy furry ones, PVA glue and spreaders.

You might want to do this activity after the Story time so as not to pre-empt it.

Spend some time touching and feeling the materials. Talk about them and try to use words which describe the look, the colour, the texture. Sort them into two piles, smooth and rough.

Give each child two circular pieces of card, or paper plates. Let them add a face to each one and then choose smooth silky material to make hair for Jacob and furry material for Esau. On the back of each you can write the name of the character, as well as the child's name. This is valuable pre-reading practice, recognising the names by shape as well as possibly by initial letter sound.

Story time

Jacob and Esau
You will need: doll and teddy dressed in Bible-style, bow and arrow, cooking pot and spoon.

Wrap the doll (Jacob) and teddy (Esau) in shawls, like babies.

Look, I've got two babies. They are twins. It's their story we're going to hear today. Shh, they're asleep. See this one, he's all hairy. He's called Esau. He was born first, so he's older. He's important because he's the older son. This one, he's Jacob. He was born after Esau, so he's a little bit younger. He doesn't like Esau being more important than him.

Let's find out what happened to them. *(Unwrap the shawls; make the toys act the story as you speak.)*

When they were little they used to play-fight. As they grew up they liked doing different things. Esau often went out into the countryside and hunted wild animals. Jacob used to stay at home and look after the sheep. He liked cooking.

As they grew older, they still used to fight!

One day Esau had been out hunting. He had walked a long way. He was tired and hungry. Back home, Jacob was making a lovely stew. As Esau came back he smelt the stew cooking.

'Mmm, that smells good. I wonder if Jacob will give me some,' he thought. 'Hello brother,' he called as he came home. 'Give me some stew. I'm hungry!'

'Only if you give me something in return,' Jacob said. Jacob dipped his spoon in and tasted the stew. 'Mmm, that's good.'

'What shall I give you?' asked Esau.

'Your rights as the older son,' Jacob said.

'I'm so hungry!' Esau replied. 'You can have my rights as the older son. I can't eat them.'

So Jacob spooned out a big bowlful of his stew and gave it to Esau. Later Esau was cross that he had given away his older-son-rights to Jacob. But it was too late then. Jacob had tricked Esau.

In the end these two brothers were such bad friends that Esau wanted to hurt Jacob! Jacob ran away to a far-off land where he would be safe.

After many years, Esau and Jacob wanted to be friends again. Jacob started to go back home. Esau set out to meet him. When they met they hugged each other. The fighting and tricking were over at last. Jacob and Esau were friends. Just like brothers should be.

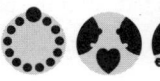

Rhyme time

Yes, yes, yes
Teach this rhyme. The children can join in by saying and nodding the 'yes' response and pretending to do the things in the verses.

Story verses:

Did Jacob love Esau?
Yes, yes, yes.
Did Esau love Jacob?
Yes, yes, yes.

But they fought and they tussled,
And they tricked and they lied,
And Esau got so angry
Jacob ran away to hide.

Did Jacob love Esau….

So they hugged and they kissed,
And they promised to be good,
They learnt to love each other
Just like brothers should.

Did Jacob love Esau….

Today verses:

Do I love my brother?
Yes, yes, yes.
Do I love my sister?
Yes, yes, yes.

We won't fight, we won't tussle,
We won't trick and we won't lie,
We'll try not to get angry,
Or make each other cry.

Song time

Teach the following song to the tune of 'Frère Jacques'. (If children know the name of the tune, tell them that 'Frère' means 'brother' in French!) Learn the song by children echoing each line. Then repeat and add in the thumb actions. To make this more fun they can have faces drawn on their thumbs and a hairy head added with a piece of fur fabric on double-sided tape.

This is Jacob, this is Jacob,
(Hold up one thumb.)
He's a boy, he's a boy,
Esau is his brother, Esau is his brother,
(Hold up other thumb.)
They are twins, they are twins.

After the children have sung the song about Jacob and Esau, it can be adapted for each child in the group who has a sibling.

This is Sarah,
She's a girl,
Sophie is her sister,
They're not twins.

Pray time

Dear God…
You will need: cut-out paper shapes of boys, girls and babies, backing paper, glue.

Ask each child to take a cut-out shape for each brother or sister they have. (Those who haven't got siblings can pray for friends or other family members: make sure they are not excluded or feel left out.) Write the names of their siblings on the shapes. Then, in turn, stick them onto the backing sheet which has 'Dear God, bless our brothers and sisters.' written on it. After sticking, each child can say 'Thank you God for…' using their siblings' names. Then everyone can join in with 'Please bless them, Amen.' Finish by asking God to help us be good to our brothers and sisters and all our friends.

Extra time

• As each child arrives make a point of asking about other members of their family.

• Sing 'Esau and Jacob', *LACH*, p24

Adults too

Sibling rivalry is known in most families. Could the adults find time to study the story of Jacob and Esau to find out what happened partly as a result of their parents' favouritism? It might be a good idea to produce a handout with Bible references, questions and suggestions, either for the adults to take home or to spend time working through together. Is it possible to gather the adults while the children are all occupied during the rhyme and song time for example? You might want to invite your pastor, an older person, or someone else from your church to guide a discussion along the lines of 'How do we foster good relationships between our children?'

Suggested format of Bible study or worksheet:
What causes sibling rivalry? Many things, but see Genesis 25:28 for a possible cause of the tension between Jacob and Esau. How long lasting was this tension? See Genesis 26:34 – and this wasn't the end. The family split lasted well into adulthood, but not for ever – reconciliation came. Genesis 33:1–16.

See *The Parentalk Guide to Brothers and Sisters* by P Spungin and V Richardson (Hodder and Stoughton).

Top tip

This story is a vivid example of what can happen when there is favouritism. We should be conscious of the need always to be fair in our dealings with children. It is easy to react too quickly to one child when another comes to us in tears and says something's not fair. We need to know the facts before we act and our action should be to help the children to resolve their conflict themselves.

Ensure that 'only' children do not feel excluded from this session.

ACTIVITY PAGE:
The photocopiable activity page for this outline is on page 54

14 God gives us families
Sisters
Miriam

Exodus 2: 1–10

Play time

Just like me
Set up a home corner and encourage the children to play the part of a 'big' sister who helps look after a baby sister or brother using the toys available. A sister will often look like her sibling in some way and so it would be good to provide dressing-up clothes. Create an activity around this: a pair of children have to find similar clothes to dress up in which will make them look alike, eg both wearing a hat, a skirt and carrying a bag rather than both wearing exactly the same clothes.

Face paints – Make up two children to look alike, eg they could both have a star on their cheeks. Use good quality paints, with adult supervision.

Hair care – Give two children similar hairstyles or hair décor. Provide hair-slides, clips, brushes, combs, ribbons and bobbles. Make sure they are washed before and after use.

Water play
Fill a large container with water. Make sure there is plenty of adult supervision and towels! Gather together a collection of small plastic boats and margarine tubs (DIY boats!) and as many small play figures as possible (Playmobil and Fisher Price figures are ideal). Float the boats and add the people: some can have 'families' of figures in the boats with one or two parents, a brother and a sister, or several sisters. Talk about what they might be doing: are they going to land at the other side and have a picnic? Are they going to row? (Some tubs can have a flat craft stick stuck on to each side and can literally be 'rowed' by the children.) Some 'boats' can be blown across the water. Perhaps one of the figures falls out of the boat and has to be rescued! The children will be able to imagine other scenarios.

Game time

Let's go together
The game is based on the idea of siblings (in this case, two sisters or brother and sister) going shopping together. Divide the children into pairs. Have scattered around the room (on the floor and on chairs and tables) various items of play food and clothing. Give the first pair of children a large shopping bag with two handles. They hold a handle each and mustn't let go. With their free hand they have to collect the 'shopping' and put it into the bag. Younger children can simply gather up the items; older ones will enjoying running round doing it as quickly as they can whilst the children watching count 1…2…3…

Making time

Lots of sisters
You will need: glue sticks, lengths of different coloured wool, fur fabric, crayons, small shapes that can be used for eyes, nose and mouth, sheets of coloured paper, small lengths of fabric and chenille wires.

Each child can make at least two cardboard roll puppets, to be sisters for each other.

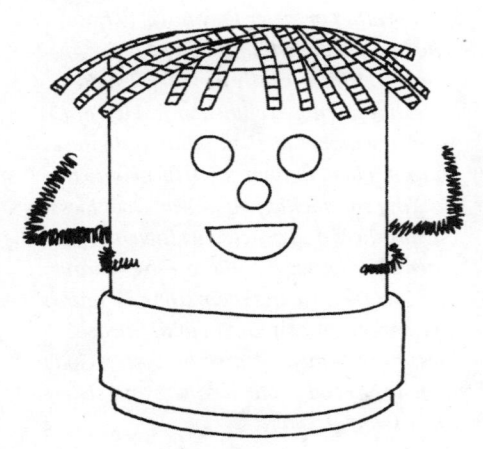

Cut up cardboard rolls into different lengths and give each child two or more if they want to make several. Decorate the rolls to make the characters. Sit alongside the children as they make their puppets and chat with them as they work.

Baby Moses
You will need: cooking chocolate, crisped rice cereal, bowl, large and small spoons, paper cake case, fondant icing.

Be alert to allergies, safety and hygiene. An adult must melt the chocolate and everyone must wash hands and work on clean surfaces.

Melt the chocolate and use it to coat the cereal. Press this into paper cases to form basket shapes. Give each child a piece of icing to shape into a baby. Put the babies in the baskets!

Story time

Big sister Miriam
You will need: a crown, basket, baby doll, paintbrush and a collection of 'children' for the beginning of the story made from cardboard cylinders.

Make the children different heights so that one is 'older' than the other. (See 'Making time'.) You will need six modern ones and two Bible-style.

Anna has a big sister called Beth who sometimes takes her to the park to play.

Arthur has a little sister called Phoebe. Sometimes he pulls her around the garden on her tricycle.

Benjamin has a half-sister called Molly. They have the same daddy but different mummies.

Miriam had a baby brother called Moses.

They lived a long time ago when there was a bad king. *(Put on a crown and pull a mean face.)* The bad king didn't like baby boys. Miriam's mummy was frightened that the bad king would hurt Moses. She had an idea.

She found a basket. *(Produce a basket – a shopping basket, a small bread basket or even a 'Moses' basket!)* Then she got some sticky tar and painted it on the bottom of the basket. *(Mime this with a paintbrush.)*

52

No water could get through now; it was like a little boat. She put baby Moses in the basket. *(Put a doll in.)*

Miriam and her mummy went down to the river. They hid the basket in the big rushes at the side.

Miriam stood and watched Moses. Then, she saw the princess. The princess had come to swim in the river. Can you swim? Let's all pretend to swim. *(Mime.)*

When she was swimming she saw a basket. What could it be? Was it a picnic? No, it was a baby! The princess thought that he was a lovely baby. She wanted to keep him *(Hold doll tightly.)* but she didn't know how to look after babies.

Moses' sister Miriam *(Show the Miriam puppet.)* knew someone who did. She told the princess, 'I know someone who will look after the baby for you.' The princess was pleased. 'Go and get her,' she said.

Who did Miriam know who could look after babies? Her own mummy! And her mummy was Moses' mummy as well! So Moses' mummy looked after her own baby.

Wasn't Miriam a good sister? She had looked after her little brother. God was pleased because Moses was going to be one of his best friends when he grew up.

Rhyme time

Rock-a-bye Moses

Explain to the children that they are going to hear a lullaby rhyme. A lullaby is a quiet song that you sing to a baby. It has to be said softly so that the baby won't wake up.

Rock-a-bye Moses fast asleep,
(Arms rocking.)
Stay there in the rushes without a peep.
(Fingers on lips.)
Your sister is watching always close by,
(Hands above eyes.)
So hush baby Moses, in the boat where you lie. *(Arms rocking.)*

Also

'Moses', verse 1, *LACH*, p26
'Baby in a basket', *LSS*, p29 and 'Baby Moses', *LSS* p30

Song time

Poor Miriam

Enjoy playing this ring game together. The tune is 'Poor Jenny sits a-weeping'.

Children walk round in a circle holding hands; one child sits on the floor in the centre, head in hands. Sing:

Poor Miriam is crying,
    is crying, is crying,
Poor Miriam is crying,
    her brother might die.

Children continue in the circle, centre child has hands above eyes. Sing:

She watches by the river, ...
    to see that he's safe.

Children still hold hands but raise arms as they walk round; centre child stands up with arms in the air. Sing:

The princess comes and saves him, ...
    his sister is glad.

Centre child joins the circle and all skip round. Sing:

Now Miriam is happy, is happy, is happy,
Now Miriam is happy,
    God kept Moses safe.

Pray time

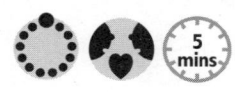

Float-a-prayer

Give each child a square of paper that has been folded as shown. Open up the flaps and let the child draw a picture, within the smaller square defined by the fold lines, of someone in their family they want to say thank you to God for – perhaps their brother or sister if they have one. Fold the flaps back over again to hide the drawing.

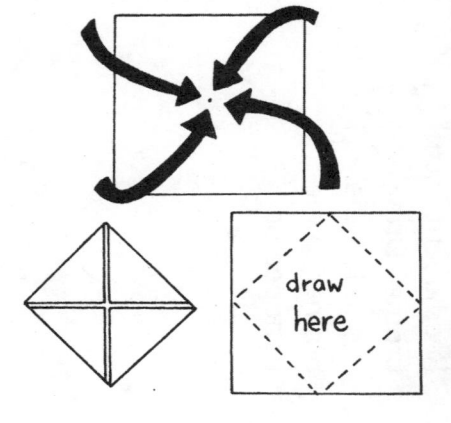

Put a bowl full of water in the centre of the group of children. In turn, lay the paper on the surface. Watch as the flaps open up and reveal the picture beneath. Explain that they are giving their prayers to God. Encourage the child to say thank you aloud for the person in the picture. God knows that they are there and will listen to them. Do not leave the children unattended with the water bowl.

Extra time

• *Dogger* by Shirley Hughes (Red Fox) is a lovely story (available in big book format) about a sister's sacrificial love.

• Count how many sisters there are in the room: don't forget to include the adults!

Adults too

Miriam's mother must have been so pleased that Miriam was concerned for her little brother's safety and didn't feel angry about giving up her own plans in order to look after him. It feels good when our children get on with each other. Family relationships can be such a help and support when good, and so crippling when bad. Sometimes rifts and hurts between brothers and sisters go back to childhood and remain unresolved for years. If appropriate, explain that sometimes situations like this are prayed for in a special time of 'prayer for healing' in the church. Anyone can come along. Sometimes it is just the first step in starting to unwrap years of bitterness and mistrust. Offer to pray with or for the person yourself: you may feel their problems are beyond you, but your concern will mean a lot to them.

Top tip

Young children love an element of surprise. If you are using visual aids for your story, don't let the children see them until the appropriate time. Cover a box with holographic or other decorative paper so that it looks attractive and the children will wait in anticipation for the next thing to come out of 'the box'!

ACTIVITY PAGE:
The photocopiable activity page for this outline is on page 55

Genesis 25: 19-34; 27:33

My name

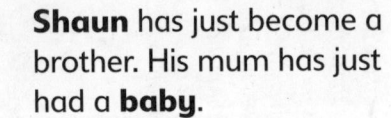

Esau and Jacob were twin brothers.

Who is a brother? Read about each brother. Draw a line to link the brother to the right person.

Esau had a brother called **Jacob**. They were twins but they did not look alike.

Peter has a twin brother called **Craig**. They look exactly the same.

Josh has two older sisters called **Hannah** and **Sophie**. He is their brother.

Shaun has just become a brother. His mum has just had a **baby**.

54

My name

Miriam watches her brother Moses to make sure he is safe.

Exodus 2: 1-10

Can you find baby Moses? Can you find his sister Miriam hiding? What else can you see hiding in the picture?

55

15 God gives us families
Families
A family believes

John 4: 43–54

Play time

Family play
You will need: doll's house and dolls, toy animals, toy town, Duplo, sets of things for sorting and matching.

Set out toys which encourage imaginative play around families or miniature worlds: dolls, families of animals, a toy town and Duplo with people.

Any activity that involves sorting things into sets helps build the concept of things belonging together and being like each other. A family is a particular set of people. Activities such as threading beads, fitting jigsaws, and sorting encourage classifying skills and help children see connections, likenesses, differences and distinctions.

Doll's house
Make a house and dolls with the children, or provide them ready-made. A simple doll's house can be made of four shoeboxes, fixed two up, two down, and covered with suitable paper. Furniture can be made out of smaller boxes and dolls out of chenille wires. The children can make clothes for the dolls out of scraps of material, if you make the dolls during your time together. Talk about who they are and where they go in the house to encourage vocabulary and concept building. Let the children play freely with the house and dolls.

Photo booth
You will need: camera (instant if possible. Otherwise, organise this during the preceding session to have the photos available on time), display board, pens.

Have a corner set up for taking photographs. Take small group photos of the children with their parents and carers. Stick the photos on a display board. Talk about how we all come from our own homes, and arrive with some people who look after us and then soon find our friends to talk to and play with.

Game time

Happy families
You will need: 'Happy families' cards.

Make a simple happy families game, or find one with clear pictures and show the children how to match the children with their parents. Using pictures of dogs with puppies, chickens with chicks and sheep with lambs as well as people of different races gives lots of opportunity for talking and matching, which is a valuable pre-school skill. Talk about which baby goes with which mother, and let the children pick from the whole set. Depending on the age of your children you may want to deal the cards out and ask for help in making a whole set, but remember that small children find it hard to play structured card games. Learning to wait for a turn is also a valuable social skill that this kind of activity can teach in a fun way.

Making time

Photo albums
You will need: stiff paper or thin card to make zigzag albums, pictures to stick on the front, pens and glue.

In advance, make an example of a family photo album for your own family. Show it to the children and talk about the people in it. Encourage them to talk about their families. Who would they have in a family photo book? Help them to make their own.

Help them to fold paper in a zigzag. Stick a bright picture on the front and write the names of people the child wants to put photos of, one per page. They might want to include themselves. (Only use capital letters for the initial letter of each name.) Tell them that they can take their photo books home and someone can help them find photos of the special people in their families. This will be a valuable exercise for them, matching – and reading – names to go with photos.

Alternatively, children can draw pictures of each person in their family and these can be stuck on the pages.

Story time

A family trusts Jesus
Allow time for the children to tell you all about their minor ailments. Enlarge the pictures below to help the children to concentrate on the story.

Tell the story like this:

Have you ever been ill? Sometimes children get earache or tummy ache. Sometimes they fall down and hurt themselves. Has that ever happened to you? Did someone come and help you? What did they do? You might have a plaster or some cream on the sore place. You might have some medicine or your family might take you to see the doctor.

I'm going to tell you a story about a daddy and his little boy who wasn't well. The little boy was very ill. He lay in bed looking pale and tired. He didn't want to play. He didn't want to eat. He didn't want to drink. He didn't want anything. His daddy had done all he could – special food, nice drinks, medicine. But nothing made any difference. The little boy just got more and more ill.

Then, one day, the daddy heard that Jesus was in a town some way away. If anyone could help, it would be Jesus. The daddy didn't mind how far he had to go, he rushed to find Jesus. At last he found him. It was about one o'clock in the afternoon.

'Please make my little boy well again,' the daddy begged Jesus. 'Come, please, before he dies.'

Jesus smiled at him. 'Your son will live,' he said. 'Go back home to him.'

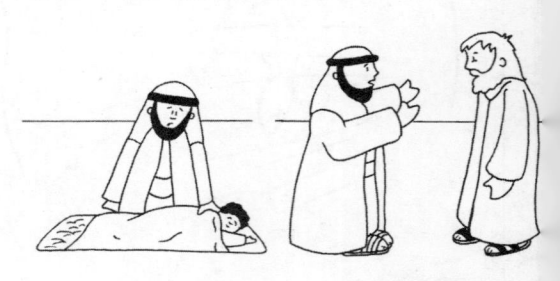

The daddy knew that Jesus meant what he said. He set off back home again. It was a long way but he didn't mind how far he had to go. On the way, he saw one of his servants running to meet him. The man had a big smile on his face. And he was shouting, 'He's better! Your son is well again!'

'When did he get better?' the daddy asked.

'Yesterday, at one o'clock. He stopped being ill! He got better all at once.'

Now there was a big smile on the daddy's face too.

'That's just the time Jesus told me he'd get better. Jesus did it.'

And when he got home he hugged his son tight.

'Now we're all going to trust Jesus,' he said. The daddy knew that the best thing for his whole family was to love and trust Jesus.

Rhyme time

A family
Teach the children this simple rhyme. If you have time, say the verse for each child, inserting the right family members in the brackets. Be sensitive to those children without various family members and ensure that they are not made to feel excluded.

A family, a family, I belong in a family,
My family, my family,
 my family belongs to me.

In my family there's (mummy),
In my family there's (dad),
In my family there's (gran and grandad),
And (one two three four) children.
Thank you God for my family,
 I belong in my family,
Thank you God for my family,
 my family belongs to me.

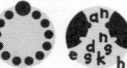

Song time

A daddy loved his son
Make finger puppets for the children to take home and use to help them remember the story. Put the little boy on the right thumb, then it can be tucked down to make it ill, the father on the right middle finger and Jesus on the left middle finger. The children can make their hands do the actions as they sing, to the tune of 'London Bridge'.

A daddy loved his son so much,
 son so much, son so much,
A daddy loved his son so much
 in Jesus' time.
(Thumb and finger moving and touching each other.)

But one day the boy got sick …
… they were worried.
(Fold thumb down into palm.)

His daddy went to ask Jesus …
… to make him better.
(Put hands together and make fingers 'talk'.)

Straight away the boy got well …
… they were happy.
(Thumb up again and all fingers dancing.)

Then everybody loved Jesus …
… they loved Jesus.
(Hands together again.)

Pray time

Our families
You will need: *a display of photographs (see Play time or make one as part of this activity.)*

Pray for each family or grouping in turn. Perhaps you could sit in a circle and ask each child and parent or carer to stand up when they are being prayed for. Remember to pray for the rest of their family. Use words like this:

'Father God, we pray for Chloe and her mum, and for her brothers at school and her dad at work. Please bless them all.'

Chant:
I love them and they love me,
Thank you for my family.

Extra time

- Make cards with the children's names on and play games helping them to find their own name. (Remember only the initial letter should be a capital.)

- More rhymes about families can be found in *Let's Sing and Shout!*, page 85.

Adults too

Very often it is only the mothers who are involved in their children's day-to-day activities. Fathers can feel isolated and out of touch. Think of ways to involve and celebrate whole families, including older brothers and sisters as well as dads. Could you organise a family fun day – a trip to a child-friendly restaurant, hire a canal boat, have a picnic, get a family film on video and a takeaway meal together? Can this become a regular part of your outreach to families?

Each *Tiddlywinks Big Book* has a special feature or event (see pages 90–91) to help you organise fun days and sessions which the wider family and friends can enjoy together.

There are many books on the subject of Christian parenting. A selection for parents to borrow would be a valuable resource. A good 'classic' book to recommend is *What is a Family?* by Edith Schaeffer (Hodder). It is not 'preachy' but full of good inspiring ideas and encouragement.

Top tip

Notice that Jesus knew the father in this Bible story could cope with not seeing the miracle happen. His faith and confidence in Jesus were strong enough. How well do we know the parents and family situations of the children we are involved with? How well do we know what each particular child needs? Pray for the wisdom that Jesus had, to give each person he met an individual response, to help their faith grow.

ACTIVITY PAGE:
The photocopiable activity page for this outline is on page 60

16 Friends of Jesus
Paul

Acts 9: 1–19

Play time

Changing materials
You will need: play dough or clay, rolling pins, plastic cutlery, pastry cutters, damp sand, buckets and spades, sand moulds.

Let the children play with the play dough or clay. Encourage them to make it into different shapes by rolling sausages or balls or flattening it with their hands or rolling pins. Create different textures on the surface using toy knives and forks. Try squeezing it through an old garlic press or cut out shapes with pastry cutters. With the sand, let the children make castles and mountains using buckets and spades or just their hands. Use moulds to create different shapes. As you play alongside the children, ask them how they are making the material different. How has the shape changed and how have they achieved this?

Dressing up
Have plenty of dressing-up clothes and let the children try them on. Do they feel different in their new outfits? Would they feel and behave differently if they were a princess/fire officer/doctor/mum? How? This fantasy play helps the children learn to understand that different people act and feel differently.

Cut and stick
You will need: background paper, magazines and newspapers, glue, spreaders.

Have a selection of magazines and newspapers with lots of pictures of faces showing different expressions. Let the children cut them out and stick them on. (Have some already cut out for the younger children. And check through the magazines beforehand to make sure there are no inappropriate images.) Talk about how our faces often show how we are feeling and encourage them to guess how the people in the pictures are feeling. This helps the children to notice visual differences and understand more about body language. Add a caption like: 'God loves us however we feel' and the child's name at the top.

Game time

Musical shapes
You will need: music on cassette player or played by adult.

Let the children dance around. When the music stops, they make a specified shape with their bodies. 'Tall like a pencil' would involve standing with arms pointing upwards. 'Small like a mouse' would mean crouching down. 'Round like a ball' would involve puffing out cheeks and curved arms. The children are exercising their bodies and thinking about how they can make them into different shapes. If there isn't much space, try making different shapes with your hands.

Follow my leader
Arrange the children in a long line behind an adult and set off marching. When the leader changes the movement the children must copy. Try jumping, walking on tiptoe, striding, going sideways, clapping as you walk. As well as developing motor skills, this encourages the children to watch closely and obey instructions in a fun way.

Making time

Paper plate puppet
You will need: unwaxed paper plates, flat craft sticks or straws, crayons, adhesive tape, short lengths of wool, glue and spreaders.

Ask the children to draw a face on each side of the plate to show a sad face and a happy face. (For younger children, have some faces ready drawn.) Add wool hair with the glue. Tape a stick or straw on the 'chin' to hold it as a puppet. Twizzle the stick quickly and you will see the expression change!

Painting faces
You will need: art paper, ready-mixed paints, brushes.

Let the children paint a face. Don't help them or do it for them but talk them through it. What shape is your face? Is your hair curly or straight, short or long? What colour is it? How many eyes do you have? What colour are they? How will you paint your mouth? Do you have a happy smile or a sad frown? Don't forget to label the paintings with the artist's name.

Story time

On the road to Damascus
You will need: long strip of paper with seven circles drawn on, marker pen.

Practise drawing the expressions as explained below. Then draw these as you speak. Encourage the children to join in making the facial expressions too.

(In the Bible, Paul is known as 'Saul' until Acts 13:9. We've called him 'Paul' throughout this section of 'Friends of Jesus' to avoid confusion for the children.)

Jesus had gone back to heaven. But his friends carried on telling people about him. They explained how he loved everyone. They said that Jesus wanted everyone to be his friends. Some people were pleased when they heard this good news. *(Draw a smiley face in the first circle.)* They believed in Jesus. Other people did not believe what the friends said. They didn't think it was true. One of these people was called Paul. He hated Jesus' friends for telling people about Jesus. *(Draw angry face: eyebrows pointing down in a V shape.)* Paul wanted to stop them talking about Jesus.

One day Paul was on a journey to a town called Damascus. Paul was still feeling angry. Suddenly he saw a bright light flashing round him. Paul was very surprised. *(Surprised face: round o mouth, high eyebrows.)* He fell to the ground. Then he heard a voice speaking to him. 'Paul! Why won't you be my friend?'

Now Paul felt frightened. *(Scared face: eyebrows pointing up and wrinkled forehead.)* 'Who are you?' he asked.

'I am Jesus,' said the voice. 'Go to the city and you will find out what to do.' When Paul stood up, he found he couldn't see! He felt even more frightened. *(Scared face again with closed eyes like little u's.)* Who was this Jesus?

Paul set off for the city, with a friend helping him. When he got there he met a man called Ananias. Jesus had told Ananias about Paul in a dream. When Ananias spoke to Paul, Paul suddenly found he could see again! *(Big wide eyes and smiley face.)*

Paul felt so happy. Ananias explained again about Jesus and this time Paul believed! He was very excited. *(Face with bigger grin.)* Paul had a new friend called Jesus who loved him even when he was angry and when he didn't believe. Now Paul wanted to meet all Jesus' friends. Paul wanted to join them in telling people about Jesus. He wanted to tell them that Jesus had changed him. His anger *(Point to angry face.)* had changed into happiness! *(Point to excited face.)*

Rhyme time

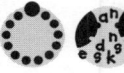

Look at me!
Repeat this two or three times and make the appropriate faces.

Can you make a face that's happy? *(Smile.)*
Can you make a face that's sad?
(Mouth turned down. Wipe eyes.)
Can you make a face that's angry?
(Frown and wag finger.)
Can you make a face that's bad?
(Pull face.)
But no matter how your face is
And no matter how you feel, *(Shrug shoulders and hold out hands, palm up.)*
God loves you now and always
(Hug yourself.)
And his love for you is real!
(Do thumbs up.)

Song time

Paul
Sing to tune of 'London's burning', repeating each phrase twice. You could make up some actions too.

Paul was angry.
Saw a light shine.
Fell down!
Jesus called him.

Paul's a kind man.
Friend of Jesus.
Hooray.
Jesus changed him.

Echo these lines, using the tune of 'Frère Jacques':

Where is Paul?
On the road,
Going to Damascus,
With his men.

Where is Paul?
On the ground.
Saw a bright light shining,
Heard a voice.

Where is Paul?
In the town.
Knows that he's met Jesus,
Very glad!

Where is Paul?
With new friends.
Knows that Jesus loves him,
Loves him too!

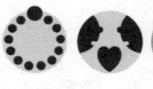

Pray time

Help us to be kind
Encourage the children to join in the prayer by covering and uncovering their eyes with their hands, to reflect Paul receiving physical (and spiritual) sight. You may need to do this several times while they grasp what to do.

We are sorry when we are angry with other people. *(Cover eyes.)*
Help us to be kind to them. *(Uncover and open eyes.)*
We are sorry when we fall out with our friends. *(Cover eyes.)*
Help us to make friends again quickly. *(Uncover.)*
We are sorry when only think about what we want to do. *(Cover.)*
Help us to share our toys and games. *(Uncover.)*
We are sorry when we don't do what you want, Jesus. *(Cover.)*
Help us to be kind like you. *(Uncover.)*

Extra time

- Share books where the main character changes, eg *Beauty and the Beast*; *The Princess and the Frog* (traditional); *The Very Hungry Caterpillar* by Eric Carle (Puffin).

- Use good quality face paints to change a child's face or expression.

Adults too

Keeping with the theme of change, why not organise a makeover session? It doesn't have to be a cosmetics evening! Be ambitious and organise a makeover of the room where you meet (with permission from the owners, of course!). This could be a great way to involve partners who don't usually attend the group. How about a morning work party, starting with breakfast together? Or a 'brush and barbecue' where renovations indoors are fuelled by a ready supply of good food outdoors?

Even if you can't decorate the whole room, you could revamp your toy storage boxes or create some cheerful wall hangings or banners which can be put up quickly at the start of the session to brighten the meeting area.

Include some books about people whose lives have been radically changed by meeting with Jesus, in your 'borrowing' area. Make sure at least some of these are contemporary as well as classics like Nicky Cruz's *Run, Baby, Run* (Hodder and Stoughton).

Top tip

Play a tape of music when it is time to tidy up. This will then become a signal for adults and children without having to cajole or shout at them! Music provides a calming atmosphere in which to tidy but can also be fun – sing along as you tidy. Encourage the children to join in with the tidying and the singing.

ACTIVITY PAGE:
The photocopiable activity page for this outline is on page 61

John 4: 43–54

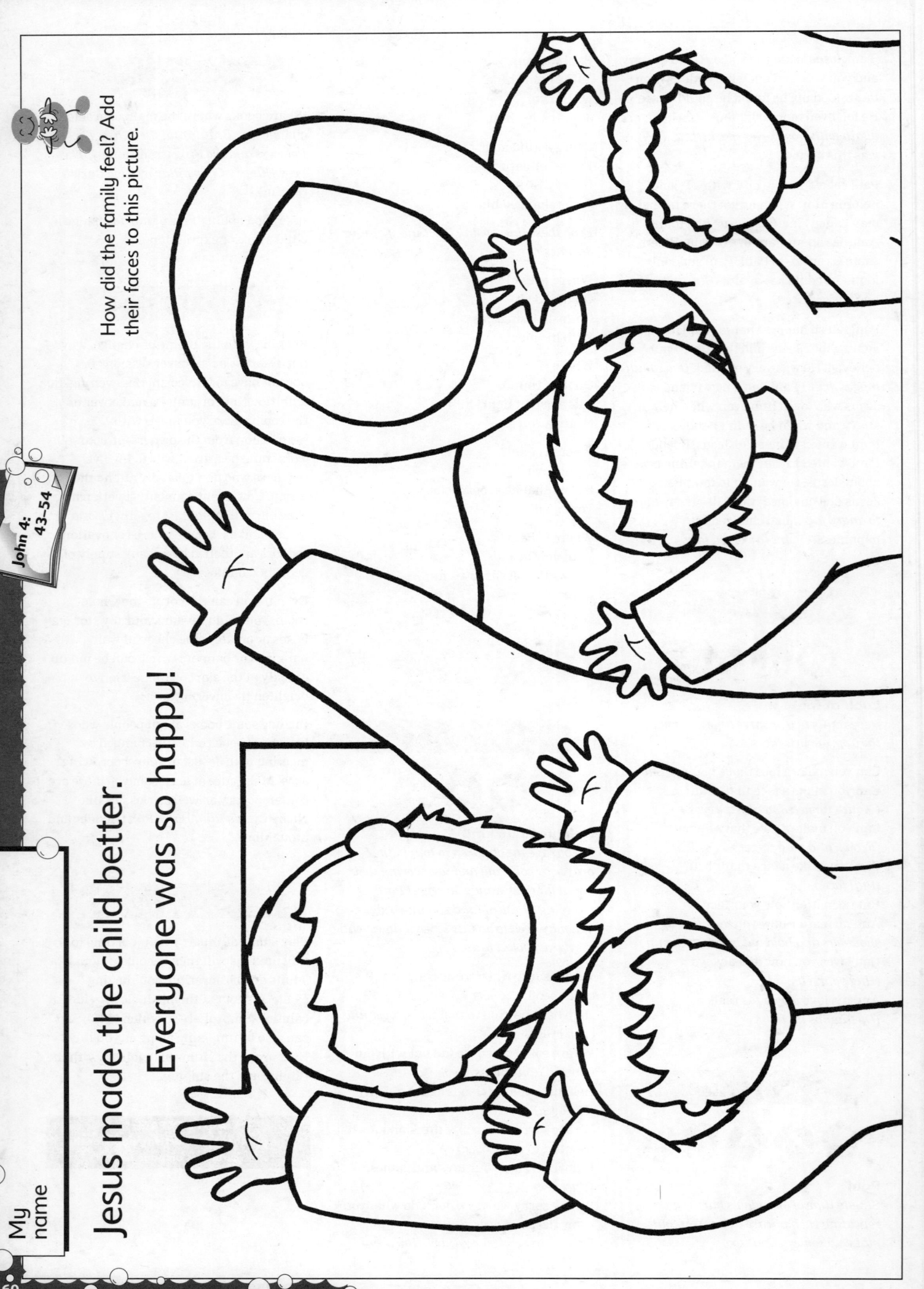

My name

Jesus made the child better.
Everyone was so happy!

How did the family feel? Add their faces to this picture.

My name

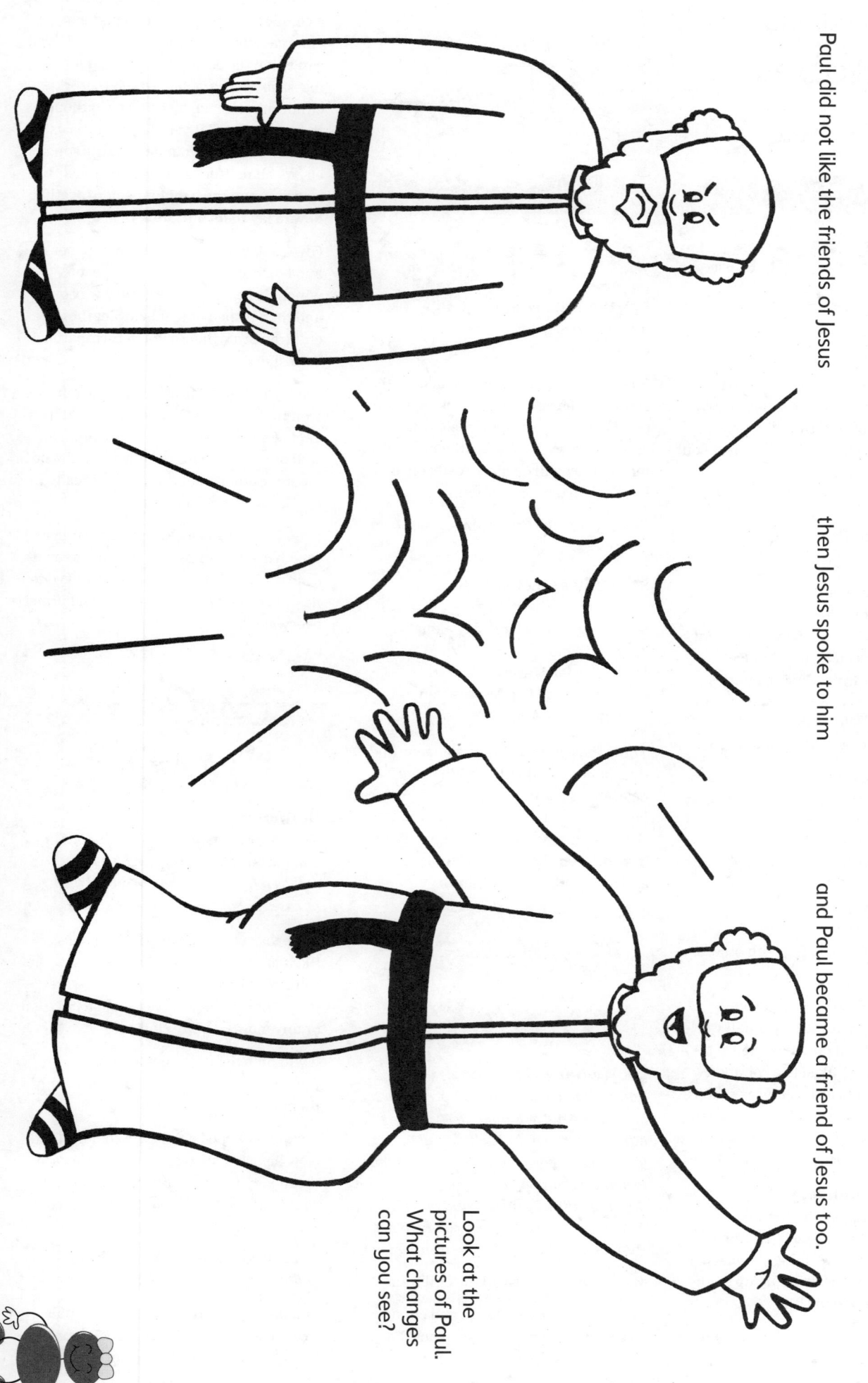

Paul became a friend of Jesus.

Acts 9: 1-19

Paul did not like the friends of Jesus

then Jesus spoke to him

and Paul became a friend of Jesus too.

Look at the pictures of Paul. What changes can you see?

61

17 Friends of Jesus
Barnabas

Acts 4: 36–37; 11:19–30

Play time

Provide free play activities which stimulate social play.

Looking on
Set out a selection of interesting safe items on a theme, eg colours, textures on a low display table. Station a helper nearby who can chat to the children about the objects. They may need to be reassured that it's all right to touch and examine – and reminded to put the items back on the table afterwards!

Puzzling time
Individual children may spend a long time working at jigsaw puzzles. Floor puzzles are particularly good for getting a number of children involved and are excitingly large scale. Choose puzzles with well-cut and well-fitting pieces and which make up into positive images. Include shape sorters and hammer toys.

Playing alongside
Activities like sand or water play enable children to play next to each other in the same sort of way with the same toys. Sitting at a table drawing, playing freely with dough, threading large buttons or reels, and sorting items by size or type means they can become aware of each other and get used to being with others.

Playing together
Encourage children to play in small groups at a common activity. Small world play works well. Set out one or more selections of toys linked to a common theme – farm, zoo, cars and lorries, doll's house, train set, construction toys. Plan your area so that very young children and babies do not have access to small pieces.

Playing cooperatively
Turn a table into a shop, with an assortment of things to sell. Let the children make believe being shopkeepers and customers. Some dressing-up clothes and bags will add to the fun.

Supervise small groups playing simple rules-based board or card games.

Game time

See the little sandy child
You will need: a floor cushion or low stool.

Place a floor cushion or low stool in the centre of the circle and choose a willing child to sit there. (When repeating the game, involve the less confident children more – they will be more ready once they have seen a demonstration.)

Chant while the child mimes their own actions:

See the little sandy girl (boy),
　　sitting on the stone,
Sighing, crying, all the day alone.
Jump up sandy girl (boy),
Wipe your tears away.
Choose a friend to play with you
　　and then dance away.

The 'sandy child' chooses someone and they dance together round the ring, before joining the circle again. It may be helpful for you to select the next 'sandy child', so that you don't end up with just a few children choosing each other again and again. Play several times.

Making time

Look what we've made!
You will need: curtain pole or broom handle (1.4–1.8 m long), 2 m strong hanging cord, plain background fabric (cut to fit the pole, top 20 cm turned under to make a channel for the pole to go through, all sides turned and hemmed if necessary), fabric crayons, coloured felt, PVA glue, white paper, iron, ironing board.

Make a banner with all the children.

Choose a phrase or slogan and cut out large letters from felt to spell out the words. (Draw the letters freehand or print out some large letters in a suitable font on a computer and use these as patterns; enlarge letters using a photocopier if you can't print large enough.) Keep the message short and one which the children can learn by heart even though they can't 'read' it yet – 'Jesus loves us' – or a line from a favourite worship song, eg 'We all matter to Jesus'. Spell the words out on the banner; decide together how to lay them out; stick in place.

Give each child a piece of white paper and fabric crayon(s). Choose crayons which can be used as ordinary wax ones and then ironed onto fabric. Let the children draw their own picture, pattern or design.

Gather in the pictures and ask an adult to iron these onto the banner, with children kept at a safe distance. (Put the hot iron well out of reach to cool down.) Slide the banner onto the pole and have it ready to display by the end of your session.

Spend some time looking at the banner together and picking out who has drawn each picture. Comment on how everyone has worked together to make it and praise everyone for their efforts.

Story time

Barnabas
Use a puppet to show what Barnabas did and to speak his words. Involve the children by asking them to repeat the phrases in bold.

Barnabas was a good man. Barnabas liked to share. One day Barnabas saw that some of the people in the church were poor. They did not have enough food to eat or any money to buy clothes.

'I will help the poor people,' said Barnabas. 'I will share what I have with them.'

Barnabas owned a field. He sold his field. Now he had a big bag of money. He gave the money to the poor people. Now they could buy food and have better clothes to wear.

'Thank you, Barnabas,' they all said. **'Thank you for sharing.'**

Barnabas was a friendly man. Barnabas liked to make friends. One day Barnabas heard about some followers of Jesus in another town. They wanted to learn more about Jesus.

'I will help them,' said Barnabas. 'I will go to their town and I will tell them all about Jesus.'

So Barnabas left his home and went to the other town. He met the followers of Jesus. He made friends with them. He met lots of new people. He made friends with them. He told all his friends how they could be friends of Jesus too.

'Thank you, Barnabas,' they all said. *'Thank you for being our friend.'*

Barnabas was a kind man. Barnabas liked to help. One day Barnabas went to see Paul. 'Come and join me,' said Barnabas. 'I need someone to help me tell people about Jesus. I think you are just the person I need.'

So Paul went with Barnabas. Soon Paul was telling people about Jesus too.

'Thank you, Barnabas,' said Paul. *'Thank you for being so kind and asking me to help you. I know this is what Jesus wants me to do.'*

Barnabas was a follower of Jesus. Barnabas liked to tell everyone he met about Jesus too. One day Barnabas heard that there were many people who did not know about Jesus.

'Let's go and tell them,' said Barnabas.

So Barnabas and Paul went to tell more people about Jesus. They went to cities and towns and villages.

Barnabas said, 'Jesus wants you to be his friends.'

'Thank you, Barnabas!' the people said. *'Thank you for telling us about Jesus. We do want to be his friends. Just like you!'*

Rhyme time

Go away... come and play

Use this rhyme informally to encourage and praise 'good' play and behaviour. Learn the second verse off by heart and try and say it to a child or children at least twice today.

'Go away, go away!'
That's an unkind thing to say.
I feel sad – it spoils my day
If someone tells me, 'Go away.'

'Come and play, come and play.'
That's a lovely thing to say!
We feel happy through the day
When our friends say, 'Come and play.'

Song time

Good friend Barnabas

Sing this song to the tune of 'For he's a jolly good fellow'.

Barnabas was a good friend,
    Barnabas was a good friend,
Barnabas was a good friend,
    and so say all of us.
And so say all of us, and so say all of us,
Barnabas was a good friend,
    Barnabas was a good friend,
Barnabas was a good friend,
    and so say all of us.

He told his friends about Jesus,
    he told his friends about Jesus,
He told his friends about Jesus
    so they knew Jesus too,
Yes they knew Jesus too,
    yes they knew Jesus too,
He told his friends about Jesus,
    he told his friends about Jesus,
He told his friends about Jesus
    So they knew Jesus too.

Also:

'Bold Barnabas', *LSS* p74
'This way, that way', *LACH* p76

Pray time

Being Barnabas

Throughout your session, be on the alert for children showing Barnabas-like qualities: working together, being friends, helping, caring, encouraging. When you see this, comment and thank the child specifically: 'Carly, thank you for letting Mark join your game. That was a kind thing to do.' It may feel artificial to you at first but this helps the children know what it is that they have done which is 'good'.

Lead the children in this prayer. First, read it to them so they know what you are going to pray. Repeat it phrase by phrase with everyone repeating the words.

Thank you, God, that I can share.
Thank you, God, that I can care.
Thank you, God, that I can be
Kind to friends as you're kind to me!

Extra time

- Tell the children (briefly) about something recent which showed you how much God loves you.

- Sing 'Everyone matters to Jesus' with actions, from *JU*, p2; 'It's great' *KS*, 175; 'God loves you' *KS*, 80; 'I belong to Jesus', *LSS*, p66

- Share drinks and biscuits by serving one another.

Adults too

Your group is thriving and you want to be friendly and encouraging, just like Barnabas, but what if you are quiet and shy and find talking to others difficult? You won't be alone! Many adults coming to a group feel awkward and their shyness may make them seem distant. Remember that you all have young children in common, and children are always a good starting point for conversation – they are bound to be doing something you can start to talk about. Being listened to is an experience which becomes rare when you are caring for young children so try to do more listening than talking.

Top tip

Help children to respond to you by using their name when you speak to them. Look towards the child and say, 'James, have you any news today?' James then knows you are talking to him and will focus on your words. If you say 'Have you any news today, James?' he will not realise you are speaking to him until he hears his name and you are more likely to have to repeat the question.

ACTIVITY PAGE:
The photocopiable activity page for this outline is on page 66

Copy this directly on to card; if that's not possible, glue Barnabas to card and cut out.

18 Friends of Jesus
Timothy

2 Timothy 1:5–8

Play time

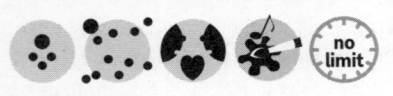

All about Jesus
Prepare a book corner, with an adult 'reader' in attendance. This is to parallel Timothy's early life and have an older person to tell the children about Jesus. Select and display some books about Jesus, if possible featuring different artwork, different sizes and shapes of books, children's Bibles and single story books. You may also have individual pictures or posters to prompt the telling of a story. Talk to the children about what the adult does.

Puppet play
Make Bible-story stick puppets, cutting character shapes from stiff card and taping them to a length of smooth bamboo or an art straw. Position the stick with the handle either at the head or the feet end of the puppet so the puppeteers either sit down and hold the puppets up, or stand up, with the puppets downwards. Make a theatre from a large cardboard box, with one side open as the front of the stage and a hole cut in the top or bottom for the puppets to go through. Children can be involved in all aspects of the puppet making: drawing figures and creating scenery, as well as using the puppets to tell Bible stories. They can either improvise their own plays or you can tell them a story about Jesus and they can then act it out. (*How to Cheat at Visual Aids*, SU, has ideas for this type of activity.)

Come to church
Provide equipment for the children to play at going to church and hearing about Jesus: chairs, large Bible, books to 'sing' from. If they are not used to being in a church building, they will need more guidance from you, but observe their play and see how they interpret their church-going experience.

Game time

Peepo
You will need: three teddies, a well-loved one (Grandma), a large one in good condition (Mum), a smaller baby bear, and an old sheet.

Rig up a simple screen from the sheet, eg drape between two tables or chairs with a broom handle to support the top; shine a beam of light on this from behind using a strong torch or projector. Settle the children in front of the screen.

Show them the three bears and introduce them. Then take the bears behind the screen and hold them up one or two at a time so the children only see the silhouette and have to guess which bear it is. Vary this by having the bears closer or further from the light source so the silhouette will vary in size; pair up the bears in different ways; put a hat on them or show them sideways.

Making time

Friendship bracelets
You will need: strips of lightweight A4 card, approx 2 cm wide and 20 cm long, two for each child; lengths of ribbon or wool approx 50 cm long.

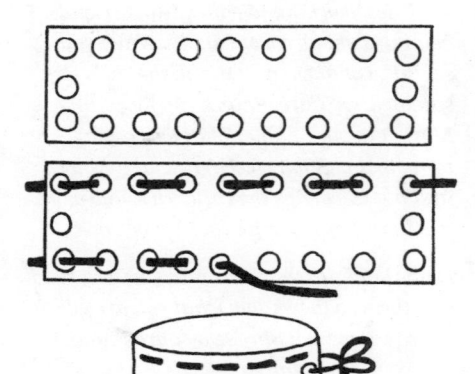

Punch holes all along the length of each strip of card. Wrap a small amount of sticky tape around the end of the ribbon or wool to make a needle, and thread in and out of the holes in the card. Leave a long length at each end to tie. Encourage the child and carer to come to the craft table together and make friendship bracelets for each other. Measure the strip of card around the wrist before starting to thread, in order to get the correct size.

Story time

Timothy
Timothy's family helped him become a friend of Jesus. This story shows how that might have happened.

It's morning at Timothy's house. Timothy wakes up and looks out of the window. 'Mum!' he calls, 'It's windy. Is there going to be a bad storm?'

Mum comes and looks out of the window too. 'It looks like it!' she exclaims, 'It reminds me of the time that Jesus and his friends were out in a storm. They were in a little boat in the middle of the sea. Everyone thought the boat was going to sink. But Jesus was asleep! So they woke him up and he told the storm to stop. And it did. Then his friends knew that he was someone very special. He was God's son!'

'Wow!' says Timothy.

It's dinnertime at Timothy's house. 'Dinner's ready!' calls Mum.

Timothy comes running, Dad comes in from work, Grandma leaves her sewing and comes to sit at the table.

'Yummy! Bread and fresh fish!' says Timothy.

'That's just like a meal that Jesus had,' says Grandma. 'One day, a big crowd of people was listening to Jesus and they were getting hungry. But there wasn't any food: just a few pieces of bread and fish. But Jesus talked to God and then there was enough food for everyone, lots and lots of people, to have as much as they wanted to eat.'

'Wow!' says Timothy.

It's bedtime at Timothy's house. Timothy snuggles under his warm blanket. Mum and Grandma come and sit beside him.

'Let's talk to Jesus, now. Let's tell him all we've done today,' says Grandma.

'And ask him to look after us when we're asleep,' suggests Timothy.

'Yes,' agrees Mum. 'He will always hear us. He knows us and he loves us and he wants to be our friend.'

'Wow!' says Timothy.

(Optional.) Timothy's grown up and he doesn't live at his house anymore.

He goes from town to town with Paul, another friend of Jesus. Everywhere they go, they tell people they meet about Jesus. Timothy knows lots of good stories about him.

'One day Jesus was in a boat on a stormy sea…' he says.

Or, 'One day a big crowd of people was listening to Jesus…'

Or, 'Jesus loves us. And he wants to be our friend.'

And everywhere Timothy and Paul go, people say, 'Wow! We want to be friends of Jesus too!'

Rhyme time

At home with Timothy
This rhyme tells of Timothy's childhood in the first two verses and his adult mission in verses 3 and 4. Use all or part of the rhyme.

Timothy lived a long time ago,
With his mum and his dad and his gran.
Mum and Gran told him all about Jesus.
'He's the best friend of all,' said Gran.

Tim was only a boy then, you see,
Just a little bit older than you.
But he knew that God really loved him
And the stories of Jesus were true.

One day a man called Paul came by.
'Come with me, and don't be shy.
Tell the stories of Jesus to all you meet,
You can do it. Just give it a try.'

So, Tim and Paul went far and wide,
Over seas and mountains tall,
And everyone
     heard about Jesus
And how he's
     the best friend of all.

Song time

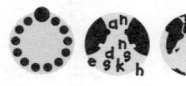

Growing and knowing
Timothy's family helped him know about Jesus. They would have told him things that we have today in our Bibles. This song, to the tune of 'Frère Jacques' explains what the Bible is and why it can help us.

What's the Bible? What's the Bible?
Do you know? Do you know?
It's God's word to help us,
To teach us and to show us,
Thank you God, thank you God.

The Bible has lots of stories in it about God's people, including ones about Jesus. Suggest you can all be like Timothy, hearing those stories today. Sing any Bible-based songs you know or choose and learn a new one.

Pray time

Who tells you?
Remind the children that Timothy heard about Jesus because his mum and his gran told him. Ask them to think about who tells them about Jesus. You will be one of the people! But are there others? (There may not be, so be aware of that.) Parents? Grandparents? People at church? At school? Other members of the family?

Give out art materials and ask them to draw or paint a picture of 'someone who tells me about Jesus'. Go round and label the portraits in clear print, eg 'Mrs Lowell at church tells Robert about Jesus.'

Either display all the pictures on a board or ask the children to hold their pictures so that you can all see them. Look around at all the people who, like Timothy's family, tell you about Jesus. Say 'thank you' to Jesus for them all!

Extra time

- Paste pictures of Bible stories (copy from this book or *How to Cheat at Visual Aids,* or draw your own) into simple scrapbooks (a few pieces of sugar paper folded and stapled together).

- Memorise a short verse of the Bible together, eg 'I love you, Lord God, and you make me strong' (Psalm 18:1). Say it lots of times and pretend to be Timothy learning from the Bible.

- Invite an experienced storyteller or puppeteer to come and present a Bible story to the children.

Adults too

The older people in Timothy's life told him about Jesus. Give the adults some suggestions for how they can do the same. Of course, one way is by coming along to your group! But you could also:

- Publicise what groups and facilities are provided by your church for this age group; have specific invitations to special events or services where children will be welcomed and catered for.

- Ask your local Christian bookshop to provide a display of resources which will help children of this age know more about Jesus.

- Suggest using *Tiddlywinks: My Little Yellow Book* which follows the same Bible passages as this book and enables children to take their first steps into Bible reading. (You can buy 10 copies at a special rate. See page 89.)

- Give Bible story books on special occasions: birthdays, leaving, group anniversary, parties.

Top tip

Have one or two children's illustrated Bibles which you can lend to children to take home for a week (*Lion First Bible* or the *Beginner's Bible*, Zondervan). Keep a list of borrowers and don't have too many Bibles available; children will be excited when it's their turn to take the Bible home and often see it as a great privilege. Try to make time to find out what they have enjoyed while they had the Bible at home.

ACTIVITY PAGE:
The photocopiable activity page for this outline is on page 67

Barnabas told his friends about Jesus.

Fold under tab

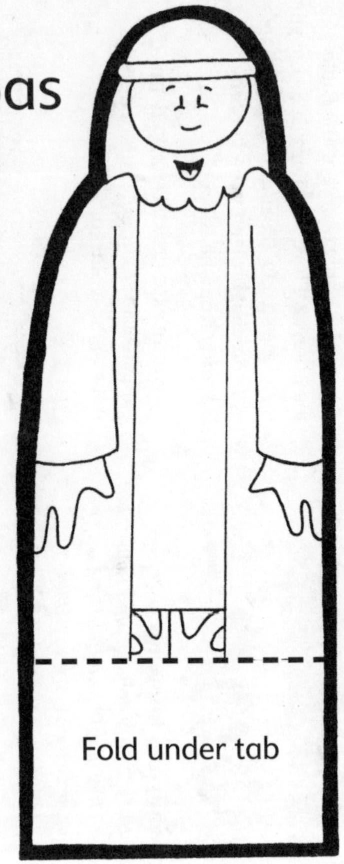

Copy this page onto card. Cut out Barnabas and fold the tab backwards so he stands up. Cut along the line. Tape both pieces together and bend along fold lines to make a zigzag, stand up scene. Take Barnabas to visit his friends and cheer them up!

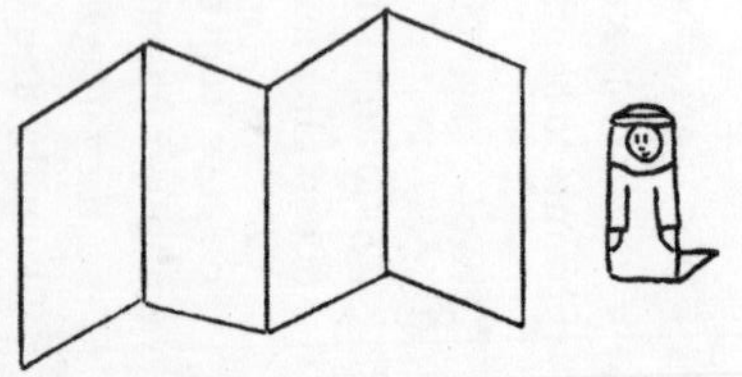

Acts 4: 36-37; 11:19-30

Barnabas told his friends about Jesus.

Barnabas and Paul went together, to tell more people about Jesus.

Barnabas shared his money with poor people.

Barnabas asked Paul to help him.

My name

My name

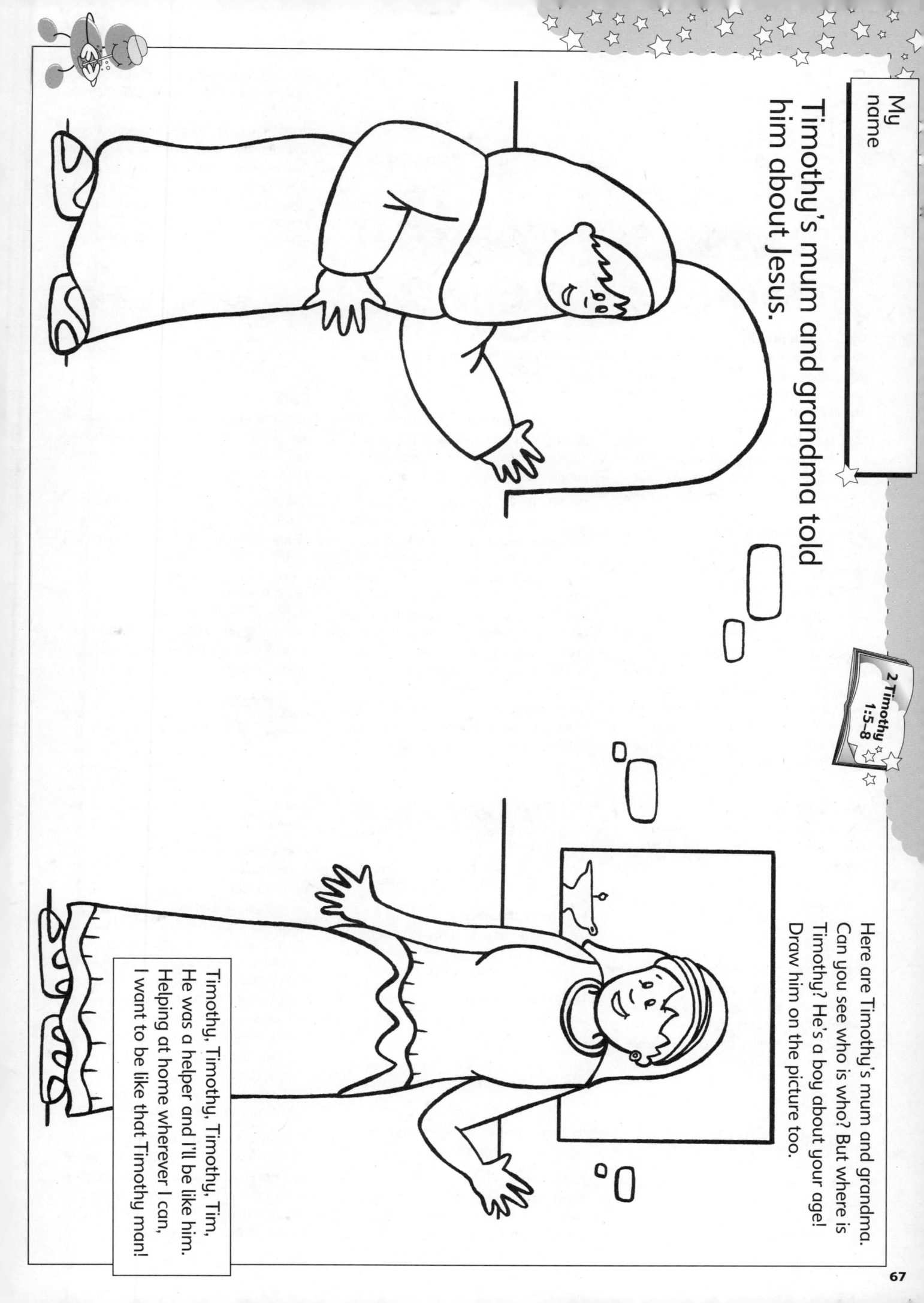

Timothy's mum and grandma told him about Jesus.

2 Timothy 1:5–8

Here are Timothy's mum and grandma. Can you see who is who? But where is Timothy? He's a boy about your age! Draw him on the picture too.

Timothy, Timothy, Timothy, Tim,
He was a helper and I'll be like him.
Helping at home wherever I can,
I want to be like that Timothy man!

67

19 Friends of Jesus
Lydia

Acts 16: 11–15

Play time

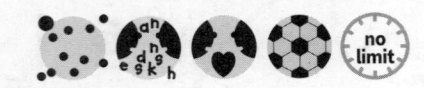

Come in to play!
You will need: large cardboard box, heavy-duty scissors, pen, playhouse, tables and chairs, kitchen equipment, tea sets, pretend food.

Make a special point of giving each child an enthusiastic welcome today. This is a good opportunity for you to make sure that you know all of the children's names! Make a pretend entrance door, out of a large cardboard box, which the children need to walk through as you welcome them. Once through the door everyone already there can give them a cheer!

Set up a playhouse or home corner, with tables and chairs, kitchen equipment, and tea sets for children to play with. Allow them to play freely, serving one another cups of tea and cooking food. Adults can enter into this time of play by calling a group of children to sit around a table with them and act the host – offering tea, coffee, milk, juice and pretend food to the children.

Wonderful welcomes!
You will need: rectangles of coloured paper approx 7 x 10 cm, sturdy plastic straws or garden cane in 25–30 cm lengths (these would cope with a larger flag), crayons and stickers for decorating the flag, adhesive tape to attach flag to straw/cane.

Seat the children at tables and allow them to decorate a flag shape and then tape it to a straw to make a flag. When all flags are made, get the children to form two rows facing one another. Let each child (and carer if necessary) take it in turns to walk down through the rows of children while the others cheer and wave their flags.

Ask the children if they enjoyed cheering for their friends when they arrived, and when they waved the flags. It's fun to make others feel welcome!

Game time

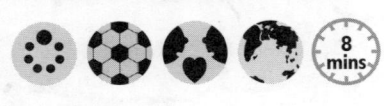

Musical hugs!
You will need: a cassette/CD player, a tape of nursery rhymes or other suitable music.

Each child should play this game with the parent or carer with whom they attend. If adults do not stay, adapt the game to simply wave or speak a greeting.

Explain that this is a game of 'musical hugs'. You will play some music and they can dance around but when the music stops they must stop and stand still. Then they need to copy an action to say 'hello' to their carer. Demonstrate a variety of ways we can do this. We might hug each other, shake hands together, kiss on the cheeks – Italians and Swiss do this three times! We might bow low like the Japanese, or do a 'Namaste' (Hands together as in prayer held out in front of you either in front of face or chest and bowing from waist.) like Indians.

Making time

Hands and faces!
You will need: ready-mixed washable paint in a tray, paper, cover-up and clean-up equipment, felt-tip pens, scissors, glue.

Beforehand write out the following words on a couple of pieces of paper and photocopy one for each child:

'Here are my hands. Let me use them to help somebody feel welcome, happy and loved.'

'Here is my smile. Let me use it to help somebody feel welcome, happy and loved.'

Explain to the children that today we are thinking about how we make people feel welcome when they visit us. To do this we use our hands and faces. Show them the sheets you have prepared as above and read out the words to them. Tell them that they are going to use the paint in the tray to make handprints on one sheet of paper and then after their hands are clean again they can draw themselves smiling on the other. How could you use these to make others feel happy? Give them to friends? Make a montage of them and display them in your group? Take them home?

Story time

Lydia
You will need: the following five pictures. You could make simple stick puppets for Lydia and Paul and use these for added focus while telling the story.

Lydia lived in a big house (1) with her family. She sold purple cloth to rich people for them to make lovely clothes. Lydia felt very happy; she had a lovely house, a lovely family and lots of money too. God had blessed her in many ways so she liked to sing songs and pray to him to say 'thank you' for all she had. She used to meet with her friends every week down by the river to sing and pray to God.

One day Lydia went down to the riverside (2). That day there were some new people there. Lydia always liked to be friendly so she said, 'Hello'. One of the new people replied, 'Hello, I'm Paul and these are my friends. We have just arrived in this town and we thought we might be able to meet other people who love God like we do.'

'Please join us,' said Lydia. So they did. Lydia and her friends sang songs, and prayed as they usually did, but they listened to Paul tell wonderful stories about Jesus too. Have you heard the story about how Jesus fed a big crowd of people with just five loaves of bread and two fish? (3) Or the time when Jesus walked on the water? (4) Lydia felt happy hearing the stories about Jesus and wanted Jesus to be her friend too. She wanted to hear more about him so she asked Paul and his friends to come and stay at her house. 'Will you come and stay with me?' she asked Paul and his friends.

So Paul and his friends went to stay at Lydia's house (5). She had lots of rooms and lots of servants to cook and look after everyone, and she was happy to share all God had given her with her new friends who loved Jesus.

Lydia said, 'God gave me a big house, now I have a busy house, sometimes a very crowded house, but it is always a happy house and that's the way I like it!'

Rhyme time

5-7 mins

Lydia and Paul
Recite the following poem and encourage the children to copy your actions:

Here are Lydia and her friends.
(Hold one hand upright and wriggle fingers.)
Here is the flowing river.
(Lay other hand flat and ripple fingers.)
They love to sit upon its banks
And pray and talk together.

Here comes Paul with his three friends,
(Move four fingers along.)
Down to the flowing river.
(Ripple fingers of the other hand as before.)
They join the women on the banks,
(Hold hands with palms facing and wriggle fingers.)
And sit and talk together.

Paul talks of his friend Jesus.
(Hold up forefinger.)
Lydia listens well.
(Cup hands to ears.)
Then she says, 'I'd like Jesus
To be my friend as well.' *(Point to self.)*

Lydia is happy. *(Smile.)*
Jesus is her friend.
(Cross hands over chest.)
'Come and stay with me,' she says,
(Beckon with forefinger.)
To Paul and his three friends.
(Hold up four fingers and then cover them with the other hand.)

Song time

3-5 mins

One, two, how are you?
You will need: a number chart or board/large sheet of paper and a marker pen.

Improvise a tune for the following words to the rhythm of 'One, two, buckle my shoe'.

Point to the numbers on your chart as you say the rhyme, as this will help the children with number recognition.

One, two, 'Hello, how are you?'
(Offer hand in a handshake.)
Three, four, 'Come in through the door.'
(Open an imaginary door.)
Five, six, 'Here's a seat, come and sit.'
(All sit down.)
Seven, eight, 'Would you like
   tea and cake?'
(Mime drinking and eating.)
Nine, ten, 'Please visit again!'

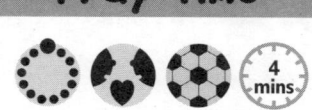

Pray time

4 mins

Two little eyes
All seated in a circle, explain to the children that we are going to thank Jesus for all the parts of our bodies that help us make people feel happy and welcome. Say the following rhyme with appropriate actions and after each line say together, 'Thank you Jesus oh sooo much!' and stretch arms – one to the floor, the other to the ceiling.

Two little eyes to look at friends,
Thank you Jesus oh sooo much!
Two little ears to hear them talk,
Thank you Jesus oh sooo much!
Two little lips to smile with them,
Thank you Jesus oh sooo much!
Two little feet to go for a walk,
Thank you Jesus oh sooo much!
Two little hands to hold their hands
Thank you Jesus oh sooo much!
And one little heart to give my love.
Thank you Jesus oh sooo much!

Extra time

• *Alfie goes to a Party*, S Hughes, Red Fox: see how Alfie feels about meeting people.

• Try saying 'Hello' in other languages.

• Ice, decorate and wrap plain biscuits for the children to give to their visitors or to take as a gift if they are being visitors.

Adults too

Discuss in the group whether people feel the communities in which they live are friendly and neighbourly. Do they feel part of a community or isolated? Do they know their neighbours or others in the street? Do they feel there are people with whom they have opportunities to stop and chat? Some of the group may have new neighbours in their locality that they have not spoken to yet. How could they get to know them a little? Or they may be new to the area themselves and feel cut off from their neighbours. Are there community groups to join? Or local events to support? Or pressure groups working for a cleaner safer environment? How can your group and/or your church be supportive?

Top tip

Think about the way in which you welcome all those who attend your group. Do they slip in quietly without being noticed? Or do they get a genuine welcome on arrival? Do you know the names of all the parents and carers as well as the children? Is there time to offer people a quick cup of tea or coffee on arrival so that you can have a little chat with them before the activities begin?

ACTIVITY PAGE:
The photocopiable activity page for this outline is on page 72

20 Friends of Jesus
Priscilla and Aquila
Acts 18: 1–4, 18–28

Play time

Free play
You will need: toys that encourage cooperative play, eg playhouse and equipment, garage and road set with cars; see-saw, huge cardboard boxes.

Set up activities that several children can take part in alongside each other and which encourage cooperative play. In the playhouse have a tea party set out with chairs and places for four people. In the dressing-up box make sure there are clothes to encourage role play. In the big equipment area, provide a see-saw. Set up a garage with a road system and lots of cars. Include any other activities you can which invite more than one child to play at once. Watch and comment on cooperative play and friendly actions.

In the box
Large cardboard boxes can be obtained from furniture stores or other shops. They have endless play value, as big boxes are irresistible to small children. Allow free play. Watch how they cooperate, follow each other's ideas and imagine the boxes to be different things.

Give the children tasks to complete. Can they build something with the boxes? How many children can get in at once? Does it make a difference which box?

If you also have small boxes you could cut doors in them so the children will have their own houses to decorate and use to retell the Bible story with their own toys at home.

Game time

Bean bag throwing
You will need: bean bags.

This is a good for improving coordination. (Throwing a ball is much harder than throwing a bean bag.) You will need to have the children standing very close together to enable them to catch the bean bags. It will also help the children to learn each other's names.

Ask the children to stand in a circle and then give bean bags to three or four of them. Call out 'Susie, throw to Peter,' etc. Make sure each child gets a turn to throw and catch.

From time to time you could ask the children to change places as well so they get to stand by and throw to different people.

If you have different colour bean bags you can ask the children to throw the red bean bag to someone who is wearing red. They need to say or point to who that is before they throw so that the catcher is ready. One bean bag can go all round the circle by being thrown to the next child with that colour on. There is lots of opportunity for learning and using colour vocabulary here.

Traditional games
Play traditional singing games – 'Ring a ring o' roses', or 'The farmer's in the den'. These encourage social behaviour and there is always a lot of laughter as 'we all fall down'.

Making time

Made for sharing
You will need: melted butter, syrup, cocoa powder, crispy rice cereal, petit four cases, bowls and spoons for chocolate crunchies; melted chocolate, small pieces of fruit, cocktail sticks, greaseproof paper for chocolate fruit.

Both of these recipes are easy to do and fun but need an adult to prepare the melted ingredients in advance. Check for food allergies. Make sure the children have washed their hands.

Chocolate crunchies
Have melted butter, syrup and cocoa powder mixed in a large bowl. Let the children take turns to stir in cereal. Make sure this is really well mixed in – it always takes more than you expect! Help the children to spoon the chocolatey mix into tiny cases.

Chocolate fruit
Let children dip pieces of fruit into melted chocolate. Put them on greaseproof paper to set.

Later, talk about what fun it was making the things together and enjoy sharing them.

Story time

Good friends
You will need: dolls or soft toys, a house made from a cardboard box with a door cut in one side.

Use the toys to act out the story and do explain that 'Aquila' is a man!

Aquila and Priscilla had a new home in a new town. They were excited. It had all the room they needed to live in, to have friends to stay and to do their work. Aquila and Priscilla made tents. They cut the material and sewed it up and made good strong tents for people to live in.

'I'm glad we moved to this town,' Priscilla said one day, as they were sitting and sewing pieces of fabric to make a tent. 'It's nice here, and we can tell lots of people about Jesus.'

'Yes, and we made a good friend when we met Paul, didn't we?' agreed Aquila.

'Yes, I hope we see him again soon.'

There was a knock at the door. Aquila went to open it.

'Oh, good, it's our new friend Paul,' he said. 'Come in, Paul. We were just talking about you.'

So Paul came in. He looked around. He saw they were making tents.

'I can make tents too,' he said. 'I'd like to work with you sometimes. But first I need somewhere to stay.'

'Stay with us,' Priscilla said. 'We love to have friends to stay and you can work with us too.'

So Paul stayed and worked with his good friends Priscilla and Aquila. Together the three of them told the people in the town all about Jesus.

One day, Aquila and Priscilla set out for the meeting place to meet all their friends. When they got there, they saw a stranger. He was talking about Jesus.

'Listen, he's a friend of Jesus, too,' Aquila said.

'But he doesn't seem to know a lot about him,' Priscilla replied. 'Shall we invite him home and tell him what we know?'

'What a good idea,' Aquila agreed. He went across to the young man.

'Come to our house and we will teach you more about Jesus,' he said.

'Oh, yes please,' said the young man. 'My name is Apollos and I'd love to stay with you.'

So another new friend came through the door into the lovely new home. Priscilla and Aquila were so happy that they had lots of new friends who loved Jesus and who would be their friends too.

Rhyme time

Jesus is my best friend
Learn this rhyme by saying it over several times. The youngest children can learn the chorus (first stanza), while older ones may memorise it all.

Jesus is my best friend,
   my best friend, my best friend.
Jesus is my best friend,
   he's with me all the time.

He's with me when I'm happy,
He's with me when I'm sad.
He's with me when I'm good,
And even if I'm bad.

He's with me in the daytime,
He's with me in the night.
Though I cannot see him,
His love will hold me tight.

Song time

God's love
This is a 'golden oldie' which children still love.

Stand the children in a circle and ask them to hold hands. Walk round slowly singing the song. Show them how there is always room for one more in a circle. The tune is 'Puff, the magic dragon'.

God's love is like a circle,
   a circle big and round,
And when you see a circle,
   no ending can be found,
And so the love of Jesus goes on eternally,
For ever and for ever,
   I know that God loves me.

Jesus loves us
This repetitive song is easy to learn and is sung to the tune of 'Bobby Shaftoe'.

Clap your hands for Jesus loves us,
Clap your hands for Jesus loves us,
Clap your hands for Jesus loves us,
What good news this is.

Wave your arms…
What good news this is.

Jump for joy…
What good news this is.

Pray time

Friends with Jesus
You will need: paper circles, crayons, backing paper, glue.

Give the children each a circle to draw a face on. Some may be able to write their names too. Have a large sheet of paper with the words 'friends with Jesus and with each other' written in the middle.

Sit the children in a circle with the large paper in the centre. Help children to stick their paper face on the backing paper. Say this thank you prayer for each child as they do so. 'Thank you for … (name). We're glad they're our friend.'

Extra time

- There are lots of picture books which deal with friendship in many different ways. Visit your local library and find a selection. Have a nice cosy story time.
- Look through magazines for pictures of children playing together. Make a collage to talk about.
- Play very simple card games together.
- Have sweets or stickers to share out.

Adults too

As Christians we are encouraged in the Bible, in stories such as today's as well as in direct teaching, to invite and welcome strangers into our homes. Taking people at face value is important as it is only if we accept others that we can expect to be accepted ourselves. Yet, the fact is that we live in, and the children are growing up in, a world where danger is often hidden behind a smiling face. A known person, more often than a stranger, may bully or abuse or even kill children with far too much frequency. So we need to teach the children how to be safe in all circumstances, while not destroying their faith in other people and in God's protection. All children's workers should be police-checked and known to be safe, but we can also teach children how to be aware and to develop personal safety skills. Make sure the parents and carers of your children know that your church follows child protection guidelines, and give them a copy of *Keep them Safe* designed for parents to use with their own children. Produced by 'Kidscape', this is obtainable from CCPAS (Churches Child Protection Advisory Service) PO Box 133, Swanley, Kent, BR8 7UQ (30p each UK). For helpful information and advice log on to www.ccpas.co.uk

Top tip

Small children do not really understand friendship in the way we do. A friend can easily turn into a rival when two children both want the same toy. Learning to share, take turns, play together is a valuable lesson in socialising. We can encourage it by emphasising the good and ignoring the bad, (unless intervention is really necessary for the safety of the children). Opportunities to play side by side without friction are the first step in learning to play together. Doing things all together is another good way of helping children to develop social skills.

ACTIVITY PAGE:
The photocopiable activity page for this outline is on page 73

Lydia said, "I want to be a friend of Jesus."

Acts 16: 11–15

Panel 1: Lydia is happy. Jesus is her friend. "Come and stay with me," she says, to Paul and his three friends.

Panel 2: Paul talks of his friend, Jesus. Lydia listens well. Then she says, "I'd like Jesus to be my friend as well."

Panel 3: Here comes Paul with his three friends, down to the flowing river. They join the women on the banks and sit and talk together.

Panel 4: Here are Lydia and her friends. Here is the flowing river. They love to sit upon its banks and pray and talk together.

Cut out these pictures and put them in the right order to tell the story of Lydia.

My name

72

My name

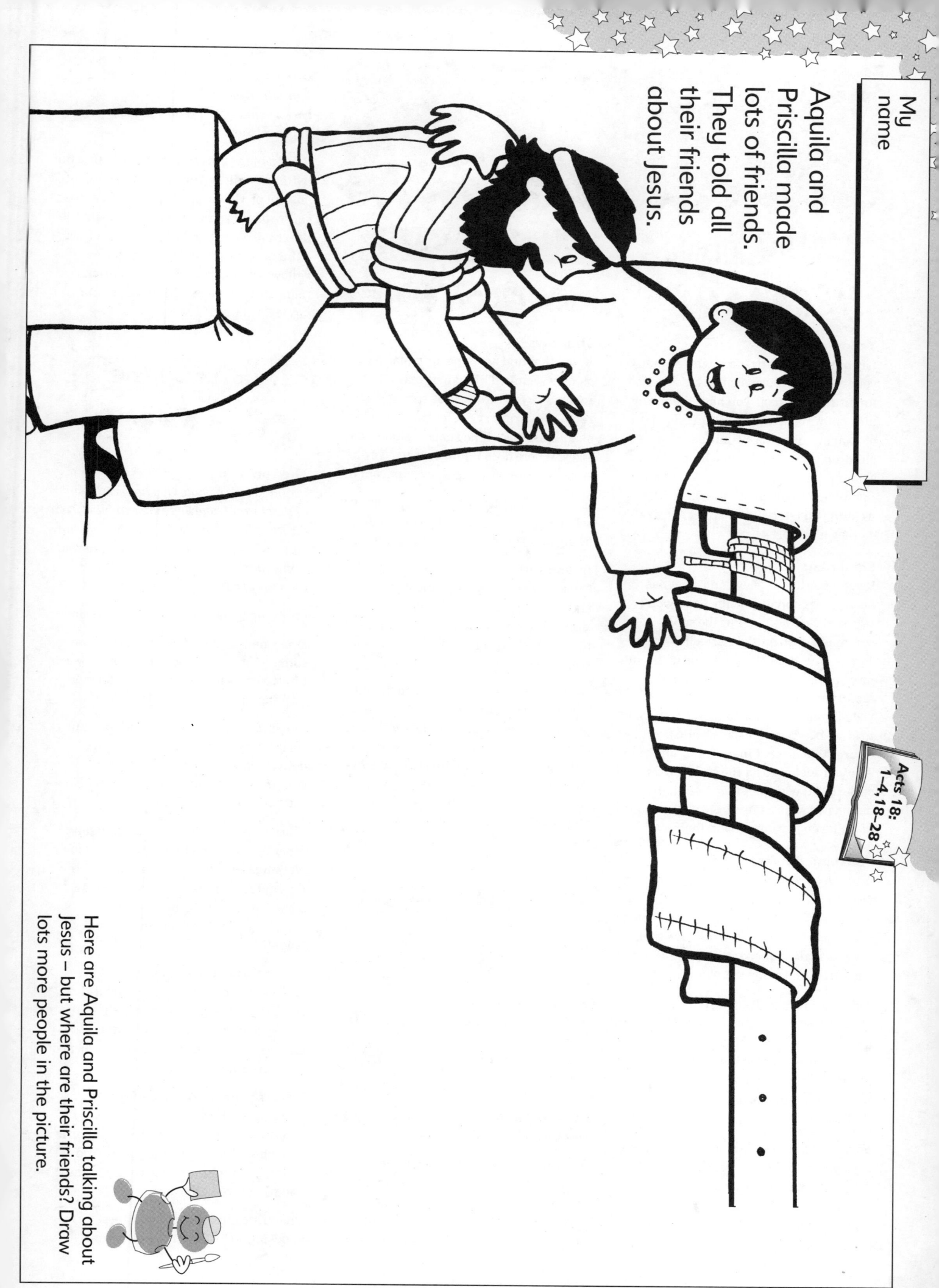

Aquila and Priscilla made lots of friends. They told all their friends about Jesus.

Acts 18: 1-4, 18-28

Here are Aquila and Priscilla talking about Jesus – but where are their friends? Draw lots more people in the picture.

73

21 What's the weather like?
Sun

Psalm 19

Play time

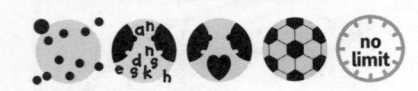

Yellow
Lay out a 'yellow toy' area with as many yellow toys as you can supply. Use yellow furniture or mats if you have them. Set up a painting area with a limited palette of 'warm' colours. Encourage the children to paint the sun with these colours. Mix a little washing-up liquid into ready-mixed paint. It helps with the washing up later and washing paint off clothes is easier!

Sand play
Remember to use 'play sand' as it has been professionally cleaned and won't stain clothes or skin. Put the sand container in an outdoor area if convenient. If so, then take the usual sun precautions. If you have no sand play facility, try using new cat litter trays or washing-up bowls for the sand. Use small toys such as pots, teaspoons and any play figures that are not in pristine condition! Another idea is to let the children use odd socks to fill with the sand. Use slightly dampened sand as this lessens the chance of children getting sand in their eyes.

Sunshine flowers
You will need: empty yoghurt pots or small plastic tubs, flower arrangers' 'oasis', sticky tape, non-toxic yellow flowers and greenery. (If getting fresh flowers is not practical, make some from crêpe paper with art straw stems as an extra activity.)

Trim the oasis to fit in the pots. Make a grid of tape across the top so that flowers can be pushed through into the oasis. (Rinse any 'dust' from the oasis off hands promptly, it can irritate skin.) Trickle in a little water afterwards, if using fresh flowers.

You will need to keep an eye on this craft area but try to keep supervision to a minimum. Let the children enjoy and experiment with their own arrangements and designs.

Game time

Shadows
If weather and space permit, play a shadows game. This can be played indoors if you have lots of sun in your room. Children try to step on each other's shadows. Look at the shadow shapes and sizes. Where does it join onto us? Try to step on your own shadow or run from it!

If you cannot play this game indoors, try setting up an overhead projector and doing hand or other shadows on the wall.

In and out
Cut a large cloud shape from cardboard and choose children in turn to be the 'sun'. When you put the cloud in front of the child all say 'in', and 'out' for when you remove the cloud.

Develop this idea by making an 'In and Out' obstacle course using boxes, chairs, playhouses, etc. Build tunnels with large foam pieces or chair cushions. Cut holes in large boxes for crawling through. Make sure everything is safe with only supervised climbing involved. Use the terms 'in' and 'out' frequently as children travel the course.

Making time

Sunny cakes
You will need: recipe for a plain cake, ingredients, yellow food colouring, icing, paper cake cases, an adult to take responsibility for the cooking. Be sure to check for allergies.

Mix up the cake but just before putting the mixture into baking cases, swirl in some strong yellow vegetable food colouring. Don't mix it too well. Bake as normal. When cool, top with yellow icing.

Our sun
You will need: a large piece of background paper, yellow paint or yellow paper, scissors.

Paint a big yellow sun circle and cut it out (with the children or beforehand) or cut one out of yellow paper. Stick this in the centre of a large sheet of paper. Either let the children do hand prints with yellow paint or draw around their hands on yellow paper and cut these out. Stick them around the outside edge of your circle for the sun's rays.

Story time

The sun's day
Psalm 19 tells of how God has set the sun in the sky and how 'nothing can hide' from the sun. This story describes what the sun does and 'sees' on one day: adapt it to your own situation to include local features, people and events.

I'm going to tell you about the sun's day.

Every new morning God wakes up the sun that he made. The sun yawns and gets up slowly. As it does, it sees the farmer milking his cows.

The birds wake up and sing a beautiful song. The sun can see the postman delivering all the letters and a doctor coming home from working all night at the hospital.

The sun sees people opening shops and other people going to their work – some walking, some on the train, some on the bus and some in cars. There's even an aeroplane flying up above the clouds. The sun shines on it and makes it shine brightly too.

Then the sun hears a new noise. It's children! They are going to school and playgroup and toddler group. The sun smiles and shines warmly on the children. Everyone feels happier when the sun shines in the morning.

There's a woman out in her garden hanging washing out to dry. There's someone else in their garden, lying on a long chair and enjoying the sun. And there are the children splashing in the paddling pool in the park.

That little girl and her daddy are choosing some flowers for grandma outside a shop. That little boy and his mummy are taking their pet dog for a walk. Look at those big heavy bags of shopping that man is carrying home! See that cat sitting on a wall. The sun looks down and sees it all.

Later on the sun sees the children coming home again and then the grown-ups after work. The sun looks in through the windows. They are eating their dinner. Then the sun sees the curtains pulled shut across the windows as the children go to bed.

The sun is feeling tired too. It yawns and starts to go down. As it does, it sends lovely streaks of colour across the sky – a beautiful orangey-red sunset. The birds see it and sing another special song again before they go to sleep. They finish just as the sun leaves the sky.

Another day is over!

Rhyme time

Sun on my face

Using yellow paper plates (either shop bought or coloured in) tape green garden sticks to the back for handles and then add faces on the front either sticking or drawing/painting.

Hold the suns high in the sky as you chant this rhyme.

Sun, sun, hot, hot sun,
Keep us warm so we can have fun.
Sun, sun, bright, bright sun,
Light each day for everyone.
Sun, sun, beautiful sun,
Isn't it good – what God has done!

Also:
'The brilliant sun', *LSS*, p12

Song time

The sun is out
Here's a new song to learn together.

The sun is out, and the sky is blue.
The sun shines down on me and you.
It feels so warm and it seems so bright;
God is the one who gave us light.

You could also sing the popular songs:
'The sun has got his hat on' and 'Who's been polishing the sun'.

The sun is out
Ruth Ranger

The sun is out, and the sky is blue. The sun shines down on me and you. It feels so warm and it seems so bright! God is the one who gives us light.

© Scripture Union 2002

If some of your adults went to church as children they may remember 'Things I love' with the first verse 'I love the sun…'

Pray time

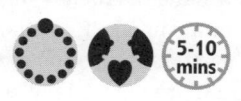

Sunny smiles
You will need: a large yellow ball (beach ball if possible), yellow disposable tablecloth.

Cut out a large circle from a yellow disposable tablecloth and get everyone to sit on it for your prayer time.

Sit the children in a circle and explain how important the sun is to our lives. God made a wonderful thing for us when he made the sun. Ask the children to pass the ball around and say a prayer to thank God for the sun when it reaches them. They may just want to say, 'Thank you, God', or they may be able to thank him for something that we can all have or do because of the sun, eg food to eat, flowers, playing outside.

Extra time

- *Peepo Sun!*, Ross and Knight, Ladybird.

- *Kipper's Sunny Day,* Mick Inkpen, Hodder.

- Bring some beach towels and spread them out on the floor, with some buckets and spades. Let everyone sit on the beach towels for circle time. Chat about sunshine, summer, holidays.

- Growing: explain how plants need sunlight to help them grow. Do some planting: cress, flower bulbs, flower or vegetable seeds, beansprouts or runner beans can all be grown easily – some in jars with kitchen paper so that roots can be observed.

Adults too

Show a clip of any science video of the sun and its properties. (Check for copyright authorisation first.) For a Christian one, try Moody Institute of Science's *Our Solar System* VC522 distributed in the UK by Sunrise Media (PO Box 300, Carlisle CA3 0QS – 01228 554342). If not using a Christian video that will say this for you, then try to make the point that God made a most incredible universe and the more we know about it the more we realise that Psalm 19 is right to say that 'The heavens keep telling the wonders of God, and the skies declare what he has done.'

Top tip

If you are able to take children out of doors for your sessions, do take all possible sun safety precautions. The sun can be deceptively strong on hazy days, so be extra vigilant. 'Slop' on sun cream or lotion (a high factor, and regularly), 'slap' on a sunhat, and 'slip' on a t-shirt (or other loose, protective clothing). Check sunglasses for scratches. Don't let children look up at the sun even with sunglasses on. Set up some kind of shade outside such as sun umbrellas and give the children more to drink than usual. Make sure children drink plenty all year round for general health and to avoid dehydration.

ACTIVITY PAGE:
The photocopiable activity page for this outline is on page 78

22 What's the weather like?
Rain

1 Kings 17:1–6; 18:41–46

Play time

Water play
Plan ahead for this activity and remind everyone to bring waterproof boots for this session.

Set up a paddling pool either indoors or outside and fill with no more than about 2 cm of water so that puddles are made. Put children into their waterproof boots and let them splash about in the watery puddles. If you are indoors, have plenty of towels around the edge of the pool for the children to step out onto! Be careful that there is not too much water which might cause the children to slip.

Put water into plastic washing-up bowls or a baby bath and let the children use flannels, sponges and towels to bath dolls and other plastic toys.

If you have water play equipment, put children in aprons and let them play with watering cans and other sprinkling toys, or supply things for them to test out floating and sinking. Add a little baby bubble bath or vegetable food colouring to the water for more fun. Never let the children play with water unsupervised.

Let the children have pretend tea parties. Children love pouring water into cups and mugs. Use trays with high sides to trap any spillages but, for hygiene reasons, watch carefully to make sure that only pretend drinking takes place!

Dry 'water play'
Make a river using blue towels/plastic sheeting/paper on the floor or a table and let the children play with toy boats on this 'river'.

Provide lots of rainwear for dressing up. If you have enough room, let the children use play umbrellas (with stubby ends) but remember that children have very little spatial awareness at this age and need more room for an umbrella than you think!

Game time

Raindrops
Set up your area with floor mats about 1 m square or large puddle shapes cut out of paper (perhaps these could be stuck down with masking tape or a bit of Blu Tack), or even draw puddle shapes with chalk on your floor if appropriate. The children pretend to be raindrops 'drip-dropping' around the room – you could use background music if you like. Either when the music is stopped or you call out 'Stop', the children must 'land' as quickly as they can on a 'puddle'. If you have arranged for them to bring their boots, they could wear these for the game.

Making time

Glittery raindrops
Let children draw their own background picture on a large piece of paper. Suggest they draw a large tree, house, car or person at the bottom of the page to leave a large area of sky. Let them dab glue on the picture and sprinkle it with glitter to show the rain falling.

Raindrop mobiles
You will need: card raindrop and large cloud shapes, crayons or glitter, glue, cotton wool, yarn.

Give each child three raindrops to colour or decorate with glitter. Guide them to tease out a piece of cotton wool and stick it to the cloud. Tape a piece of yarn to the back of each raindrop and the other end under the cloud. Add another piece of yarn for hanging the cloud up.

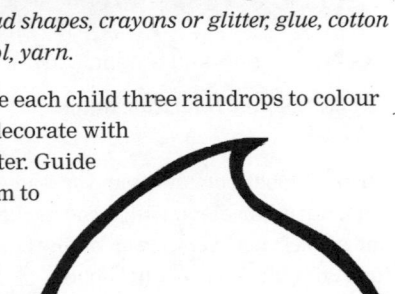

Rainmakers
Choose plastic containers that will be easy to hold; even better if they are transparent. Film cases or small plastic drinks bottles are good. Part-fill the containers with lentils/pasta/rice and stick the lid on securely with parcel tape. These can be used for any musical activities you do today.

Story time

Rain? Rain!
Use hand puppets to represent Elijah and Ahab. The children will love it if you spray the characters with some real water at the end!

Elijah was a man who loved God. But there was a new king in his country who didn't love God. His name was Ahab. Ahab did lots of unkind things to his people and didn't keep the laws that God had made.

God sent Elijah to see Ahab. Elijah said to him, 'King Ahab, God will stop the rain in your country until you change – until you start to do good things for God.' This could be very bad. With no rain, food would not grow and there might not be enough water to drink. But still Ahab would not change.

So the rain didn't fall in that country. Elijah went away to hide. You see, King Ahab didn't like Elijah. He wanted to make Elijah start the rain again. So Elijah hid from Ahab. God sent birds to bring food to Elijah while he was hiding, and he was able to drink from a clean little river nearby.

Three years went by. It was a hard life for all the people as they had no food or water. Then God sent Elijah back to Ahab. Elijah said again, 'King Ahab, you must change.' This time Elijah showed Ahab how strong and great God is. King Ahab began to realise that he should love God.

Because he was starting to change, Elijah said to Ahab, 'Go and eat your dinner because soon it will start to rain again.

The rain will be very heavy!'

Elijah sent his friend to look towards the sea for signs of the rain. His friend couldn't see anything – only a big blue sky. But Elijah knew God would send the rain soon.

Elijah sent his friend back to look again – still nothing.

Elijah sent him again.

And again.

And again.

And again. Six times he saw nothing, then on the seventh time he saw a tiny cloud! That was the start of the rain! Elijah said to Ahab, 'Leave your dinner and get back home because the rain is coming quickly!'

The cloud got bigger and the wind started to blow it towards them. The rain started. It splashed down hard and fast. King Ahab drove home in his chariot pulled by his strong horse. God gave Elijah amazing strength so that he was able to run back home faster then Ahab's chariot, to get out of the rain!

Rhyme time

Elijah and the rain
If you wish to sing this story-rhyme, it goes to the first part of the tune 'The Keel Row'.

The ravens fed Elijah, Elijah, Elijah,
The ravens fed Elijah
And God looked after him.

God sends the rain down, the rain down, the rain down,
God sends the rain down,
He knows just what we need.

Song time

Rainy day songs
Make a rainstorm using percussion instruments or your own shakers (see Making time).

Or use your 'body instruments'. Start by getting the children to rub their hands together: it's drizzling. Then tap one finger on their palms as the rain falls harder.

Then two, three and four fingers, as it gets louder. Clap at the rainstorm's loudest. You could try to reverse the sequence to show the rain moving away again.

Sing this rainy song to the tune of 'If you're happy and you know it'. Children clap on the 'splash, splash' at the end of the lines.

It's raining and Elijah's getting wet –
splash, splash!
The raindrops are falling down his neck –
splash, splash!
Puddles all around
Are splashing on the ground,
It's raining and Elijah's getting wet –
splash, splash!

It's raining very hard; I'm getting wet –
splash, splash!
The raindrops are falling down my neck –
splash, splash!
Puddles all around
Are splashing on the ground,
It's raining very hard; I'm getting wet –
splash, splash!

Pray time

Pitter patter prayers
Use sound effects as a background to your prayers – particularly of rain, rushing water, or even a thunderstorm. Give each child a paper or cellophane raindrop. As each child puts their raindrop in a bucket in the middle everyone says, 'Thank you God for rain.'

After all have done this, lead some prayers thanking God for clean water to drink and wash in, for rain to make our food grow. You might like to use this one:

Wash the floor, clean the house,
Wipe my face with water!
Feed the plants, shine the glass,
Quench my thirst with water!
Thank you, God, that there are lots
Of things to do with water!

Then tip the bucket of raindrops upside down so that they fall on the children like rain!

Extra time

- Let parents/carers know the previous week that the children can bring in their umbrellas (with 'stubby' ends). Put the umbrellas up and let everyone sit under them while chatting about their umbrellas and rain.

- Hang streamers of thin blue crêpe paper across an open doorway so you have to walk 'through the rain' to enter the room.

Adults too

Around the world it seems to be that while some areas have too much water and suffer flooding, others are suffering from drought and famine conditions. Set up a display of information or show a video from an aid agency working in drought, famine or flood-damaged areas of the world. Use the information to stimulate discussion. You may decide that you want to fund-raise for a project: if so, think about choosing a certain target to raise or a definite project to support – this can be more encouraging than an open-ended commitment.

Top tip

Rainy day books to enjoy together:

Kipper's Rainy Day, Mick Inkpen, Hodder.
Postman Pat's Rainy Day, John Cunliffe, Scholastic.
Postman Pat and the Rainy Day (board book), Mammoth.
Umbrella Weather, Hilda Offen, Happy Cat Books.
It's Rainy, Manning and Granstrom, Franklin Watts.

For some activities in this session you will need to ask the parents/carers the previous session to bring boots and umbrellas. Have a few items spare in case anyone forgets.

ACTIVITY PAGE:
The photocopiable activity page for this outline is on page 79

Where is the sun? How many other circles can you find? Colour them all in yellow.

God put the sun in the sky.

Psalm 19

My name

78

My name

Make lots of rain fall on Elijah and the King. Join the dots around the clouds. Draw in the rain or stick on thin streamers of blue tissue paper.

Elijah ran faster than the king could go in his chariot!

1 Kings 17:1-6; 18:41-46

79

23 What's the weather like?
Wind

Acts 27

Play time

Bubbles
Put a large bowl of bubble mixture on a table and the children dip their wands into the bowl and either blow or wave the bubbles out. If the children are younger, adults could blow the bubbles for the children to try to pop. This may be better done on mats or outside, in case the children slip on any spilt liquid. There are all kinds of bubble blowing equipment available. It's also very effective to dip a hand in the mixture, make a circle with thumb and forefinger and blow through this loop.

Make your own bubble mix with thick baby bath or washing-up liquid. Pour this slowly into warm water and stir carefully so that it doesn't froth up. Add some glycerine to get really good bubbles.

Blow!
Use large trays or shallow cardboard boxes to blow objects around with drinking straws. Make sure the objects are not small enough to be sucked up the straw. Try table tennis balls, tissues, corks, feathers, tissue paper, newspaper shapes.

Play 'Flip the Kipper' by cutting out paper fish shapes and wafting them across a smooth floor with magazines or table mats.

All aboard
Get big cardboard boxes for the children to sit in and use as boats. They could make their own flag or sail. You could give them kitchen roll tubes for telescopes. These boats could also be decorated by the children and used during your Story time.

Twirl and swirl
Let the children have a 'twirling' time. Ask them to pretend to be a leaf falling to the ground or twirling round and round in the wind. You could have background music as well.

Game time

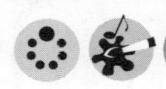

Balloons
Play with balloons, keeping them up in the air as long as possible.

Weather vane
Make sure the children have enough space to run to all four sides of the room and name these walls 'North', 'South', 'East' and 'West'. Everyone stands in the middle and the children ask the leader or selected child, 'Where does the wind blow?' The person answers and points with both arms (like the pointer of a weather vane) towards the relevant wall. The children run to the wall. The first person to reach the wall becomes the next 'weather vane'. For younger children, the running provides sufficient excitement so don't emphasise the competitive side of the game.

Making time

Blow painting
Put a spoonful of runny paint onto a sheet of paper and let the child blow the paint into patterns with a straw. Add other colours as they go along. Don't let them put the bottom of the straw into the paint and ensure they know the difference between blowing and sucking.

Fans
Make paper fans. Fold an A4 sheet of paper landscape-way round concertina-wise with folds of about 2 cm. Wrap tape across the folds at the bottom to make a handle and then spread out the top part of the fan.

Kites
Make kites by cutting across the bottom of a paper bag. Tie a 1 m length of string to each top corner. Strengthen this with sticky tape. Let the children decorate the bag and add streamers. They fly their kite by holding the two strings together and pulling the bag along behind them as they run.

Story time

Paul's shipwreck
Let the children sit in their Play time boats (if these were made, or make them now), and join in with the actions to the story.

Long ago a man called Paul went on a long exciting journey by ship. In those days ships didn't have engines. They had big sails that helped the wind to push the ship along. Some soldiers went too. *(March like soldiers.)*

At first the journey was fine, but then the wind began to blow. *(Make a noise like the wind.)*

The ship began to move faster; the wind got stronger and stronger and the waves got higher and higher. *(Make big wave shapes with your hands.)*

It was a bad storm! The sailors couldn't steer the ship. It just rocked about on the waves. *(Rock like a ship on the stormy sea.)*

The captain was worried that the ship would sink, so he told the sailors to make the boat lighter by throwing out some of the cargo. Boxes of clothes, packets of food, tools and other things the ship was carrying went overboard into the sea. *(Pretend to throw things over the side of the rocking boat.)*

The wind kept blowing and the sky was so dark that the sailors couldn't see the sun in the daytime or the stars at night. They didn't know which way they were going. *(Shade your eyes with your hands and look for the stars in the sky.)*

They were lost! Everyone began to be very frightened. *(Look scared.)*

But Paul said to them, 'Don't worry! Last night God sent an angel to me with a message. Everyone will be kept safe, but we will be shipwrecked on an island.'

And it happened just as Paul said – the ship they were travelling in was wrecked. The front hit a sandbank and the back of the ship was broken by the heavy waves. The soldiers told everyone who could swim to jump into the sea and swim away before the ship sank completely. *(Pretend to jump into the sea and swim.)*

Those who couldn't swim grabbed pieces of wood and used them to float to the beach. Everyone reached the beach safely! God had taken care of Paul and his friends and of all the people on the ship with them.

Rhyme time

Going with God
This rhyme shows some of the discoveries that Paul made: God takes care of us, is with us and makes life fun!

Journeys, journeys all the time,
Walking or on the bus –
It's good to know, wherever we go,
God's taking care of us!

Journeys, journeys everywhere,
Some near, some far away –
It's good to know, wherever we go,
God's with us every day!

Journeys, journeys, lots of them,
In wind or rain or sun –
It's good to know, wherever we go,
God's making life such fun!

Song time

Can you see the wind?
Can you see the wind? *(Blow, blow.)*
Can you see it blow? *(Blow, blow.)*
Where's it going now? *(Blow, blow.)*
Do we really know? *(Blow, blow.)*

God made the wind *(Blow, blow.)*
Made it soft or strong *(Blow, blow.)*
God made the wind *(Blow, blow.)*
Blowing us along. *(Children twirl.)*

Pray time

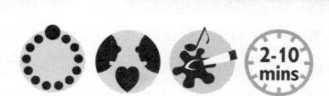

Blow a prayer
Show the children how to make a blowing noise by cupping their hands round their mouths and blowing through. Practise this a few times. Then say these words, derived from Psalm 78:26, and ask the children to blow at the end of each line:

God sends the wind from west and east,
From north and south
    through all the land.
Wherever it blows,
Wherever it blows,
It comes and goes at God's command.

Flying fish
Cut 2 cm wide strips of A4 paper for the children. Cut a 1 cm slit from the lower edge 5 cm from one end and another slit from the upper edge 5 cm from the other end. Children write their name/mark on their fish and slot them together (perhaps with adult help). The leader prays for each child in turn and they throw their fish up high making it twirl.

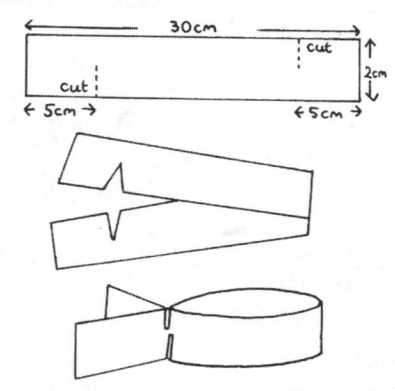

Say: 'Dear Jesus, please look after everyone here,' while all the children twirl their fish.

Extra time

- Is there a weather vane on your building? If so, go outside and look at it.
- *Kipper's Kite*, Mick Inkpen, Hodder.
- *Postman Pat and the Breezy Day* by John Cunliffe, Scholastic.
- 'Watching the wind', *LACH*, p84

Adults too

Get hold of as many different kinds of wind chimes as you can – wooden, metal, large, small, tuned to different notes, all the same note, ones with an integral beater, etc. Hang them up and let the adults have fun trying them all. It would help if a breeze were making the chimes sound while you are talking. Speak about the wind and how it can't be seen – only its effects, like through the wind chimes. Explain that the Bible describes God the Holy Spirit, as being like the wind. He can't be seen but his effects can. God changes peoples' lives for the better by his Holy Spirit. The Bible also talks about the Holy Spirit being the breath of God. Just a breath of wind can make the wind chimes sound, and the breath of God can touch our hearts and change our lives.

Top tip

Make bubble pictures using washing-up liquid in watery coloured paint. Powder paint works well, giving a 'grainy' effect. Blow bubbles into the mixture using long transparent tubing (this avoids the problem of children sucking up by mistake as you can see if the mixture is going the wrong way). Lay pieces of paper over. Make sure the pictures are dry by home time.

ACTIVITY PAGE:
The photocopiable activity page for this outline is on page 84

Can you see the wind?

© Scripture Union 2002
Ruth Ranger

Can you see the wind? blow, blow. Can you see it blow? blow, blow. Where's it going now? blow, blow. Do we really know? blow, blow. God made the wind, blow, blow. Made it soft or strong, blow, blow. God made the wind, blow, blow. Blowing us along, twirl.

81

24 What's the weather like?
Cold

Psalm 147: 15–18; Proverbs 31: 13, 19, 21

Play time

Warm homes
Have toys in a play area that are to do with homes; doll's house, Duplo or other construction toys for building houses etc. Explain that homes give us shelter to keep us warm when it's cold outside.

Out in the cold
Have dressing-up hats, supplying as many different kinds of hats as you can – not just 'cold weather' ones. Choose which to wear for different weather.

It's cold!
You will need: *gloves for the children to wear.*

Part fill clear plastic drinks bottles with coloured water and freeze. Make sure that the lid is on securely and cannot be opened by the children. Let the children put their hands near the bottles to feel how cold they are. Wearing gloves, they can handle the bottles as the ice melts, feeling the cold and how the bottle changes from being solid to being less rigid.

Snow play
Make a mixture of cornflour and water either in individual bowls or one big bowl and let the children play with this. As it changes its texture from firm to runny, see if the children can build a snowman with it. Spoons are useful to play with. Try this recipe for an individual 20 cm diameter bowl: 100–150 ml of water with 200 g of cornflour.

Multiply according to bowl size. Children's hands will need to be washed afterwards and keep an eye on them to make sure none of the 'snow' is eaten!

Watch
Ask someone who is a fast knitter to work throughout the session, making, for example, a scarf for a teddy bear. Children can observe the process and see how the item grows and the knitter can explain what is happening, how and why.

Game time

Feeling cold?
Prepare a 'cold bag'. This should contain lots of scarves, hats, gloves and big socks, (don't just put in one pair), even a big woolly jumper or two. Put this in the centre of a group of children. Pass any small object, such as a mitten, around the circle. You could use music, so when it stops or the leader says 'Stop', the child holding the object takes an article of clothing out of the bag and puts it on. You could put a rogue item in, like a pair of sunglasses or a sunhat!

Warm up!
Improvise your own warm-up dance for a chilly day. The music needs to have a very strong four-time beat with about 2 beats per second – slow enough for stepping from side to side, stretching, bending, moving forwards and back and around.

Making time

Door hangers
Make door hangers by enlarging and cutting this shape from blue card.

The children can decorate both sides with white shapes to stick on, making a 'cold' picture. Use pre-cut shapes such as icicles, icebergs, igloos, polar bears, etc.

We're cold!
You will need: *long lengths of paper (wallpaper, frieze paper), paper or fabric pieces, adhesive.*

Ask each child to lie on the paper on the floor while you draw round them or have some child shapes pre-cut. Cut fabric or paper into 'cold' weather clothing shapes so that the children can stick clothes onto their figure to make them warm. This idea could be varied by using bird or animal shapes and sticking on pretend feathers or fur to keep them warm.

Cool colours
Let the children do free painting using a limited 'cool' colour palette such as blues, greens, purples, grey, black, white.

Story time

C-c-c-cold outside…
Explain about the woman in Proverbs 31 making clothes to keep her family warm. Read verses 13, 19 and 21 from a Bible. Ask the children to listen for what she does (weaves cloth, makes clothes, gives her family warm clothes for cold weather). Explain what these processes are and today's equivalents. Is anyone wearing anything hand-made? Can you bring a knitted garment to show? If you have a knitter at work (see Play time), how is the knitting progressing?

When might we need clothes to keep us warm? Tell the children you're going to tell a story about a little boy like them. Tell the story once. Repeat it and this time ask the children to count the 'keeping warm' things in the story.

When Danny got out of bed that morning his feet felt cold. He looked under his bed for his **slippers** and put them on. Danny went downstairs to find Mummy in the kitchen. She made him some **warm porridge** for breakfast. Danny put on his **clothes**; his digger **jumper** and fleecy green **trousers**. Mummy called him over to the window. 'Look at the frost, Danny.' Danny saw funny icy squiggles and spikey patterns. He tried to touch them but they were outside. Then he saw the snow! It was lying all over the garden. Danny couldn't see the grass or mud. It was all white!

Mummy helped him to put on his **boots**, his **coat, hat, scarf** and **gloves.** She opened the back door and Danny clambered out into the snow. His foot went right down into it! He saw his footprints and his breath in the air! It was like steam! The snow was hard to walk in, so Danny stopped and picked up a handful. Brrr – he shivered. It was cold. His gloves were getting wet. The snow in his hand was turning to water.

Danny lay down on his back in the snow. He dragged his arms up and down then stood up to look. 'Mummy,' he called, 'I've made a snow angel!' His arms had made a picture of wings. Mummy brought Danny **inside**. She took his outdoor clothes off, then she gave him a **warm drink** and a **cuddle**. They looked outside at the angel. It had started to snow again. The big white fluffy flakes floated down and covered the angel. Soon it was gone but Danny didn't mind. He had had a lovely cold day.

Rhyme time

It's cold today
Use appropriate actions if you wish.

Cold, cold, God's made it very cold:
I'll put on my coat
   because my back is cold,
I'll put on my hat
   because my head is cold,
I'll put on my scarf
   because my neck is cold,
I'll put on my boots
   because my feet are cold,
I'll put on my gloves
   because my hands are cold.
I go outside with all these clothes on
And now I find that I am warm!

Song time

When it's cold
When it's cold I shiver, Brrrr
When it's cold in winter, Brrrr
Wrap up warm with lots of clothes,
From my head down to my toes.
God will bring the summer.

When it's cold
Ruth Ranger

When it's cold I shiver, brrr
When it's cold in winter, brrr Wrap up warm with lots of clothes
From my head down to my toes. God will bring the summer.

© Scripture Union 2002

On a cold and frosty morning
Enjoy the nursery classic game and song. Form a circle and walk round slowly as you sing the verse. Then stop and do the actions. Remember it's a cold morning so make sure you shiver as you get dressed!

Here we go round the mulberry bush,
The mulberry bush, the mulberry bush,
Here we go round the mulberry bush,
On a cold and frosty morning.

This is the way we clean our teeth….

Ask the children what other things you could do on this cold and frosty day and make up further verses together.

Pray time

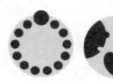

Each one different
Prepare a paper snowflake for each child. Fold a circle of white paper in half three times, cut or tear shapes out along the folded edges. (Children may want to have a go at this themselves: they need strong scissors and fingers to do this as well as plenty of help and encouragement!) One by one, give the folded shape to a child and let them unfold it and see the unique pattern. Explain that every tiny snowflake is different to every other: no two are ever the same. (Show some enlarged photos if possible.) Hold the paper snowflakes as high as you can and let them fall to the floor as you say together, 'Thank you God for the cold weather.'

Extra time

• Paint a frosty pattern, using a doyley as a stencil to dab paint through.

• If it's a cold day, wrap up warm and go for a walk together (with lots of adult supervision).

• Shake a snowglobe and watch the snow falling.

Adults too

Explain to the adults that sometimes we're all tempted to wish that the weather was different, that it was warmer or maybe that winter would be over and spring would come. Yet Christians believe that God made everything in our universe and made it to work well; which includes cold weather.

If you have the Moody Institute of Science video (see page 75), then use the end part to explain how the earth is conducive to sustaining life. God has organised the universe in such a way that the earth is within the only 2 percent of temperature differentiation to be able to sustain life. If we were any closer to the sun it would be too hot, and any further away would make it too cold. Our climate (with its cold weather as well as its hot) also helps the atmosphere to provide the water vapour necessary for life to exist.

Top tip

Chill out with: *The Snowman*, R Briggs, Puffin, Ladybird; *Little Red Train to the Rescue*, B Blathwayt, Red Fox; *Postman Pat goes Sledging*, J Cunliffe, Scholastic; *One Snowy Night*, N Butterworth, Picture Lions; *First Snow*, K Lewis, Walker Books; *Jolly Snow*, J Hissey, Red Fox; written for slightly older children, *Snow is falling* (Branley and Keller, HarperCollins) is an introduction to the science of snow.

ACTIVITY PAGE:
The photocopiable activity page for this outline is on page 85

Acts 27

My name

The wind blew. There was a big storm but God kept everyone safe.

The wind is still blowing. Point to all the places you can see the wind blowing.

Look out of the window. Is the wind blowing today? How do you know?

Warm clothes for cold weather!

My name

Psalm 147: 15-18; Proverbs 31: 13, 19, 21

This is how people made their clothes in Bible times. What is the woman doing in each picture? Colour in what she's holding and making.

What do you wear when it's cold outside? Ask a grown-up if you can put those clothes on now!

85

25 What's the weather like?
Rainbows

Genesis 9: 8–17

Play time

Rainbow dressing
Provide dressing-up clothes in as many colours of the rainbow as you can find. Children especially seem to like cloaks. These can be made from old curtains tightening up the heading tape to fit roomily and then turning this over inside the cloak, sewing it down and putting a hook-and-loop fastener on each end. Do not use tie fastenings to avoid the danger of strangulation. Longer skirts can be made simply by making a channel at the top all around a fabric tube and threading elastic through to fit. These can also be put on under the arms to make a dress.

Noah's Ark
Provide animal toys to play with. Farm animal toys are fine; even better if you have enough so that pairs of similar animals are available. Older children can select and match these pairs for themselves.

Use a large cardboard box to make an ark. Have the opening facing upwards. Cut a big doorway halfway down one side, cutting the top and sides of a hole big enough for hands holding animals to reach through. Fold the bottom of the doorway down to the ground as a gang plank. Children can use this box as an ark and put pairs of animals into it.

Rainbow biscuits
Set up an 'icing zone' where children can use coloured water icing to decorate plain biscuits. Provide rainbow-coloured sugar strands, hundreds and thousands and small jelly sweets, and 'writing icing' to add more colour and variety. Let them create their own designs and give only essential supervision. (As for any food activity, be aware of hygiene and the possibility of allergies.)

Sorting
Mix small coloured items (reels, play buttons, blocks, etc) in a big container and let the children sort them out into different colour sets.

Game time

May we cross the water?
Set up two mats or areas on the floor of your room a few metres apart (mark boxes on the floor with masking tape or chalk). The leader or a chosen child stands on one while everyone else stands on the other. All say to the leader:

'Please Jack,
May we cross the water,
In a cup and saucer,
Before we go to bed?'

The leader/child replies, 'Yes, if you are wearing the colour …' and chooses a colour.

Children wearing clothes of that colour then run across to the other mat.

Parachute games
If you have access to a parachute, especially a multi-coloured one, play some parachute games. Books of games are available to buy but the general rules are to space the children around the parachute holding the edge, and to pull tightly to bounce a ball around the upper surface, or to flap the parachute up to run underneath.

Making time

Paper rainbows
Depending on the age of your group either have bowls with torn pieces of paper separated into the colours of the rainbow, or let the children tear their own pieces (roughly 3 cm square). Children can glue these onto a piece of paper to make a rainbow. Or, as an activity for the whole group, make a very large rainbow picture for your wall.

Sun catchers
Using transparent disposable cups and a mixture of PVA glue and water (1:5), stick pieces of different coloured tissue paper or acetate on the cup as decoration. Coat the whole decoration in a layer of the glue mixture. Leave to dry upside down on a plastic sheet. Make a hole in the bottom of the cup and thread a knotted piece of string through to hang up at home.

Story time

Noah and the rainbow
Use a prism (available from toy and science shops) to throw a rainbow into your room. Move it around slowly and point out the colours. Spread different coloured fabrics or paper over the floor to make a rainbow and sit the children on it. Get the children to copy your actions.

In the Bible it tells us that a long, long time ago the world had gone wrong. People were doing horrible things. So God decided to start the world again.

God found a good man called Noah and told him how to make a huge boat. *(Show size with hands.)* Noah made the boat. *(Do lots of banging, hammering, chopping, sawing.)* God asked Noah to put two of every animal and bird in the boat. They had to bring lots and lots of food! Noah and all his family got in the boat too, and the door was shut. *(Clap hands together.)*

It started to rain. *(Wiggle fingers downwards to show the rain.)* It rained so much that the boat floated away. *(Form waves with your hands.)* After lots of days the rain stopped. The sun dried the land and everyone was able to come out of the boat.

God put a rainbow in the sky. He told Noah it was to show his promise to everyone. God promised not to flood the world with water again. Noah looked up at the rainbow. He saw the big black rain clouds moving away and the sun shining brightly again. When Noah looked at the beautiful bright shining colours of the rainbow, he felt happy. He knew God would keep his promise. The Reds, *(Children on red fabric stand up.)* Oranges, *(Stand.)* Yellows, *(Stand.)* Greens, *(Stand.)* Light blues, *(Stand.)* Dark blues, *(Stand.)* and Purples, *(Stand.)* sparkled in the sunshine. *(Look up at the sky with hands shielding your eyes, pretending to see a rainbow.)*

Rhyme time

3 mins

See the rainbow!
Lead this rhyme with everyone joining in with the words in *italics*.

There's a rainbow in the sky,
God put it there!
Look at it to make you smile,
God put it there!
Red and yellow, green and blue –
See what God has done for you.

There's a moon to see at night,
God put it there!
Great big stars are shining bright,
God put it there!
Red and yellow, green and blue –
See what God has done for you.

One big sun to see each day,
God put it there!
Lots of light to show the way,
God put it there!
Red and yellow, green and blue –
See what God has done for you.

Song time

3 mins

In the ark
Learn this new song and sing it through, adding the actions as you become more familiar with the tune.

Two elephants went in the ark, *(Arm up to nose and wave as a trunk.)*
Two elephants went in the ark,
Two elephants went in the ark,
Then they sailed away.

Two kangaroos went in the ark… *(Jump with feet together and hands together, in front of chest.)*

Two bumble bees went in the ark…
(Wiggle your index fingers around as they 'buzz' everywhere.)

Two crocodiles went in the ark… *(Hold your arms out straight in front and clap together like snapping jaws.)*

See a rainbow in the sky, *(Hold arms out high and wide and 'draw' an arc in the air.)*
See a rainbow in the sky,
See a rainbow in the sky,
God has put it there.

Make up more verses, as suggested by the children.

Pray time

7 mins

Rainbow prayers
Spread a large sheet of paper on the floor or fix to the wall (with a drip-mat underneath). Paint on coloured arcs to form a rainbow, one arc for each short prayer. This will be easier to do if you have another leader to either paint or pray. All repeat, 'Thank you, God', after each line.

Thank you, God, for the beautiful world that you have made for us. *(red)*
Thank you, God, for the fruit and vegetables to eat. *(orange)*
Thank you, God, for the sunshine. *(yellow)*
Thank you, God, for the trees, grass and flowers. *(green)*
Thank you, God, for the rain, rivers and seas, and for our clean water to drink. *(dark blue and light blue)*
Thank You God for all the animals and birds that make us smile. *(purple)*
Under the rainbow draw some stick-people and say:
Thank you, God, for our friends and families who look after us.

Extra time

- Read *Come into the Ark with Noah* by Stephanie Jeffs, SU.
- Practise naming different colours and finding items of that colour around the room.
- Sing 'Mister Noah built an ark…' (in *JP* and many other compilations).
- Cut streamers from coloured crepe paper and wave them as you dance to music.

Adults too

You might like to use or adapt the following for a brief talk:

There seem to be so many parts of the world where life has turned sour, maybe as in Noah's time. We hear constantly of wars or natural disasters and so much human suffering. We may be experiencing things like this in our own lives but next time we see a rainbow, it can be a chance to gain fresh hope. In the Bible, God promised not to destroy the world by flooding again, and he has promised to be here with us through our problems.

Give each person their own rainbow reminder (maybe a prayer card or a bookmark with a rainbow motif) of God's promise.

Top tip

Colour blindness can affect as many as 1 in 12 of all men and boys (particularly white, European). Females are very rarely affected. As very few colour blind people are 'blind' to all colours, it is often missed. Most sufferers have difficulty distinguishing between certain colours, usually reds or greens. This is worth remembering if you are making wallcharts, flashcards and visual aids for your Story time. Try to avoid using coloured texts on coloured backgrounds, particularly combinations of orange and green.

ACTIVITY PAGE:
The photocopiable activity page for this outline is on page 88

In the Ark
Ruth Ranger

Two el-e-phants went in the ark, two el-e-phants went in the ark, two el-e-phants went in the ark, then they sailed a-way.

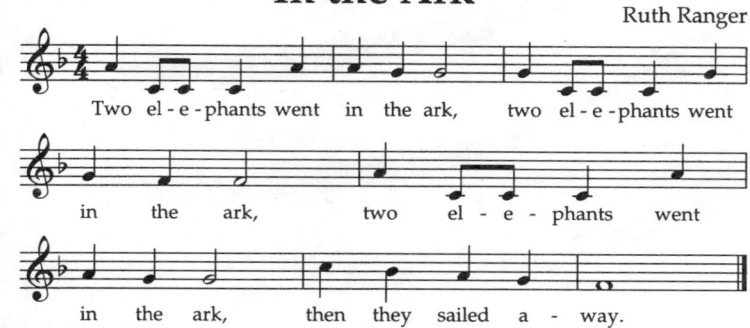

© Scripture Union 2002

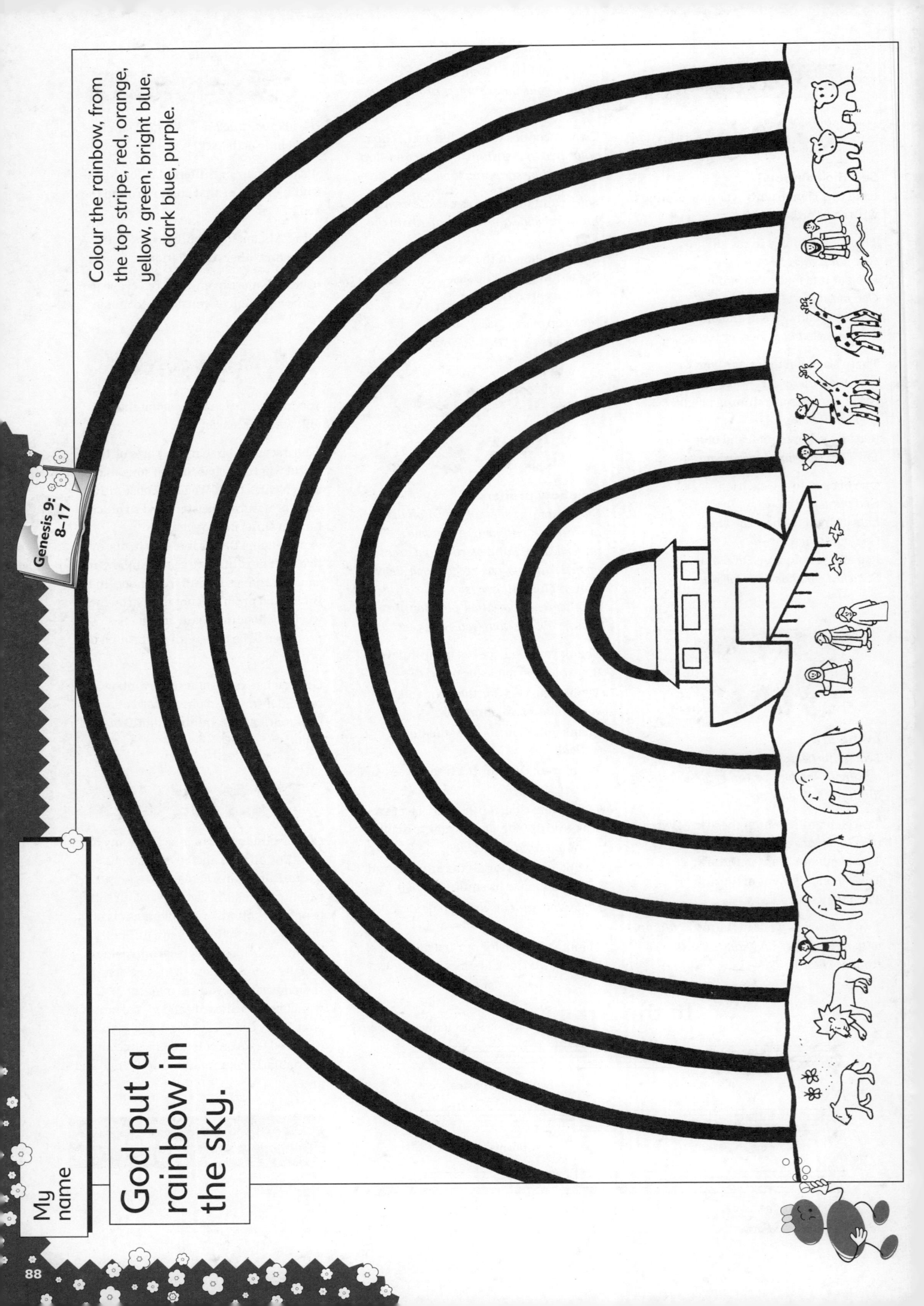

Colour the rainbow, from the top stripe, red, orange, yellow, green, bright blue, dark blue, purple.

Genesis 9: 8–17

My name

God put a rainbow in the sky.

First steps in Bible reading
The *Tiddlywinks* range of Little Books

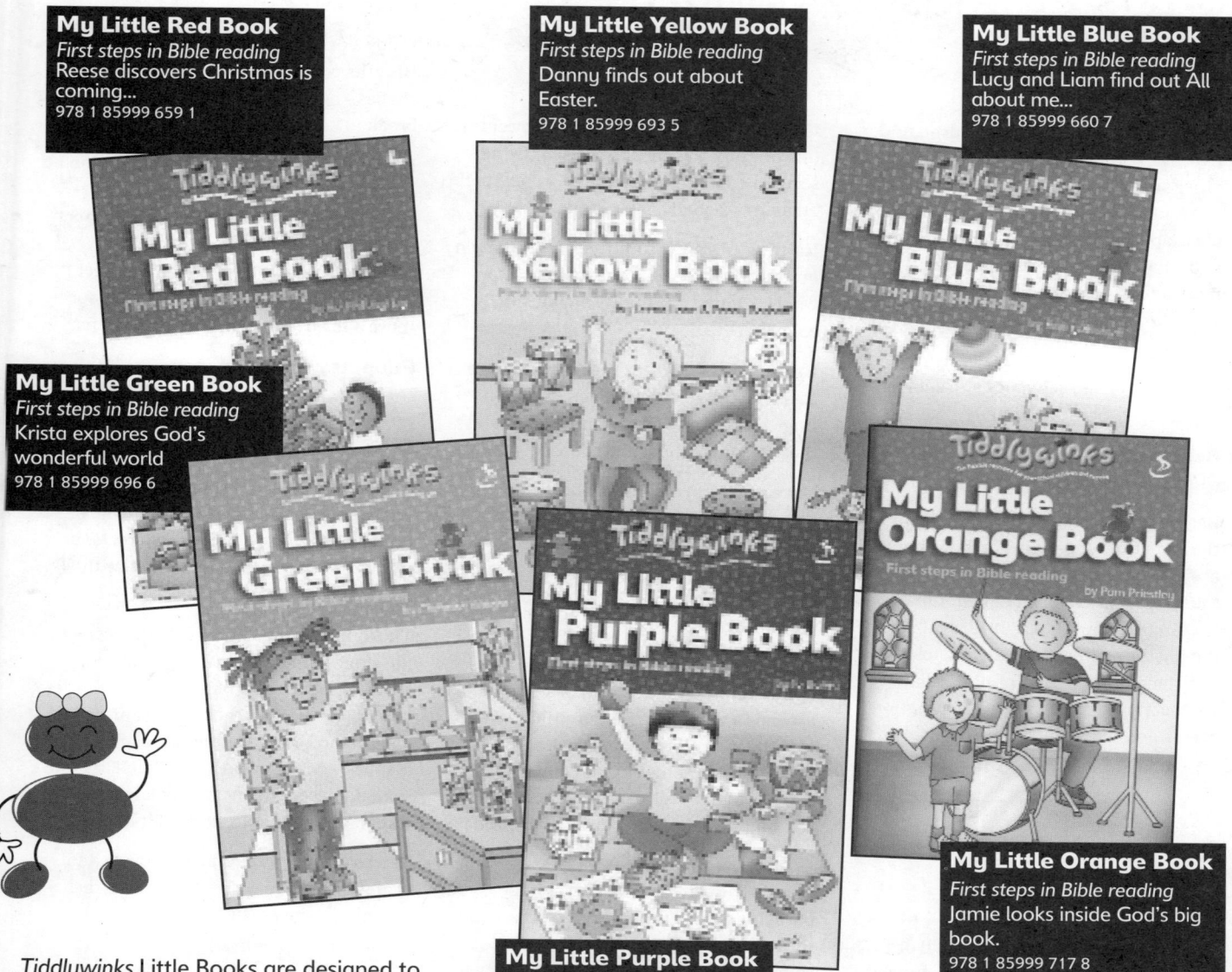

My Little Red Book
First steps in Bible reading
Reese discovers Christmas is coming...
978 1 85999 659 1

My Little Yellow Book
First steps in Bible reading
Danny finds out about Easter.
978 1 85999 693 5

My Little Blue Book
First steps in Bible reading
Lucy and Liam find out All about me...
978 1 85999 660 7

My Little Green Book
First steps in Bible reading
Krista explores God's wonderful world
978 1 85999 696 6

My Little Purple Book
First steps in Bible reading
Lily discovers 'Jesus loves me'
978 1 85999 720 8

My Little Orange Book
First steps in Bible reading
Jamie looks inside God's big book.
978 1 85999 717 8

Tiddlywinks Little Books are designed to be used at home by a parent/carer with an individual child. Linked to the themes covered in the *Tiddlywinks* Big Books, children can discover and learn about the Bible and share their discoveries with you. There are 50 first steps in Bible reading pages in each book, with a story for each day and extra activity pages of fun things to do. Children will love exploring the Bible with child characters Lucy and Liam, Reese, Danny and Krista.
A5, 64pp £3.50 each

You can order these or any other *Tiddlywinks* resources from:
- Your local Christian bookstore
- Scripture Union Mail Order:
  Telephone 01908 856006
- Online: log on to
  www.scriptureunion.org.uk/shop
  to order securely from our online bookshop

> When the Big Books are used in conjunction with the Little Books, children and adults encounter an attractive mixture of stories and activities that will encourage everybody to know and trust in Jesus.
>
> **Diana Turner,**
> **Editor of Playleader Magazine**

Tiddlywinks
The flexible resource for pre-school children and carers

Also now on sale!
Glitter and Glue. Say and Sing
Even more craft and prayer ideas for use with under fives

Easter Eggstravaganza

This event is designed for children under five years of age with their parents or other supervising adults. Children aged two and a half to four years will be able to participate effectively, children under two and a half are still included but will need more adult supervision.

The event is designed for up to 90 minutes: if you have less time available, omit some of the activities and shorten the 'Activity Stations' time.

Registration
(Allow 20 minutes, overall)

Begin approximately 10 minutes before the start time depending on how many are expected. Registration team staffs the registration area for the 20 minutes, keeping an eye out for late arrivals during the session. It is always helpful to register addresses, age of children, contact number for follow up invitation events and fire/safety regulations.

Programme

Easter activities stations
(30 minutes)

Set these areas up around the hall or in smaller rooms, using tables surrounded by chairs. Ideally they should be child-sized tables and chairs. Have each activity supervised by a team member throughout whilst children and 'their' adults rotate around the creative stations, running simultaneously. A sample of each activity is a good idea, but children should be encouraged to express their own ideas. Parents/carers can assist children creating, and finish off if a child requests it. Creations should be named, if possible for identification, for collection later and left for display on table around the side of the meeting area, as the programme moves on.

Organise up to five stations:

Easter egg – Draw a giant Easter egg on A4/A3 paper, using a bold black line. Give children self-adhesive coloured stickers to create their own designs, supplemented by colourful washable marker pens (with ventilated tops).

Flowers – Draw a large simple flower on (minimum) A3 stiff paper. Decorate using scrunched up coloured tissue paper stuck on using washable glue sticks.

Rabbits – Draw the outline of a rabbit on large stiff paper; decorate using cotton wool for tails and chunky crayons to colour in the body.

Cross – Draw a large cross in the centre of a sheet of A3 sugar paper. Put out finger paints and let the children use these to add pattern and colour.

Cave and door – Using coloured play dough, children make a cave with a circular door.

Parachute
(10 minutes)

Mushroom the parachute and call a child's name or age as the parachute ascends and encourage the child to walk into the middle and come back again before the parachute comes down and catches them. This can be great fun and can highlight that God loves each child and knows us by name.

Place a balloon for each child on the parachute and see how high you can flap the balloons in the air. Children can, at some point, go under the chute and try to knock the balloons off. For under-fives, adults kneeling works best. The balloons could be imagined as bouncing Easter eggs.

For a separate activity bring the chute over your heads, down your back and sit on it. One adult stands in the middle as a tent pole. Children can wave to each other inside the ballooned shape or you could use the time to sing songs. You could mention how, in the Easter story, a man will be placed in a cave but will come alive again, so let's come out of the chute…

Find footprints
(5 minutes)

Find small animal footprints that have been hidden around the room. These can be hidden beforehand or during the parachute game. It is done to time and it is not essential every footprint is found as long as each child has found at least one. Adults can assist if needed.

Refreshments
(5 minutes)

Enjoy a drink and a biscuit together. Biscuits could be home-made in 'Easter' shapes – egg, cross, chick. Have a short break to keep the programme moving.

Keep children out of kitchen areas, don't carry trays of warm drinks into areas where those under five are playing. Sit the children down on a mat for their drinks. Use feeder beakers for younger ones and plastic cups (only half-full) for those a little older.

Puppets and visual story
(10 minutes)

Using an animal puppet like a wolf, sheep or dog, invite the children to come and sit in a defined area. The puppet tells the Easter story from the point where he has been woken up by a noisy cockerel (sound effects included). Plan and practise this beforehand.

The animal puppet describes the scene in the story using these key objects: sun, cross, empty cave, door of cave, sad/happy face. As these are mentioned, place appropriate simple visual on a large display board. Cover this with felt and put a small piece of loop-and-hook fastener on each small picture to hold it in place.

'It was a hot day, the sun was lovely and orange, it was very crowded and in the morning, very noisy.

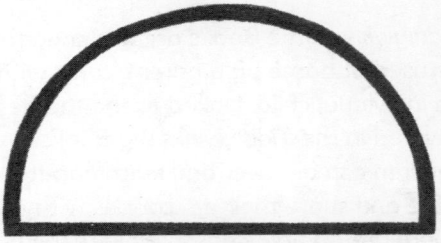

In the afternoon it was quieter and I was going for a walk and saw the man on the cross.

Lots of people were looking at him. Many had sad faces and were crying. When I went back later when it was quieter, some men were taking him down to a cave.

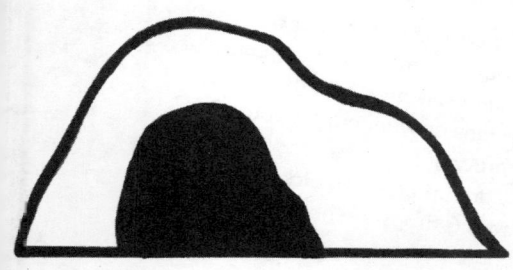

I watched them roll this heavy stone in front of the cave.'

After this point in the story, ask the children to walk or run around and then sit down again. (You could do this three times.)

The puppet explains that after he had spent three days running around, he found the cave door open and no one was inside when he looked. He then saw many happy faces *(face turns to become a happy face)*.

On asking why people were so happy, he found out that the man who had died was called Jesus and he is alive again. Hooray!

Balloon dancing
(3 minutes)

Give inflated balloons to everyone. Explain that the friends of Jesus were happy to know he is alive so let us try to be happy and do something that makes us smile! Play some happy music and tap the balloons into the air, seeing how long you can keep them there. Make sure there is plenty of space for this, and remind adults to help children avoid bumping into one another.

(Some young children are frightened of balloons, especially if they burst. Be aware of this and sensitive to any anxious children.)

Music
(7 minutes)

Celebrate Easter with song, music and movement. Adults can sing these kneeling, to be at the children's eye level.

Choose from:

'The butterfly song',(If I were a butterfly), in many compilations.

'Jesus' love is very wonderful', *JU*, p14

'God's not dead', *JU,* p38

'Sing a song, sing a joyful song', *KS,* 297.

Lids game
(8 minutes)

Divide the children into groups of six.

A tray is brought to each group with lots of coloured large bottle or jar lids. Under half of the caps is an edible sweet, eg a chocolate raisin or jelly bear. The children take turns to turn over one cap at a time. If they discover a sweet underneath they can eat it or give it to an adult for safe keeping until afterwards. The children should have a minimum of two turns each (more if necessary to ensure they all find a sweet).

Easter collage
(10 minutes)

Make smaller versions of the visual aids used for the story. Give each child a set and a piece of pale blue A4 card/paper. Adults help only where necessary to help children glue their objects onto the card. Each object is a simple shape and different colour. It doesn't matter if the children do not get everything positioned right!

Party bag
(3 minutes)

Give out bags containing something to eat (a mini Easter egg or a packet of chocolate raisins or buttons) and a little book to tell the Easter story. We recommend *Jesus Lives* (Little Fish, SU) and *The First Easter* (Bible Pebbles, SU). Have a mix of titles so that siblings don't have the same.

Top tips

- Check your venue is safe for under-fives. Pay particular attention to eye and head level sharp objects, cupboard corners and trailing wires. Keep doors shut onto car parks or roads.

- Prepare well beforehand, collecting items in advance, buying resources, having the right amount of team members to run the event effectively.

- Design your programme to be varied, colourful and flexible.

- Advertise your event appropriately with suitable flyers given out a minimum of two weeks in advance.

- When using puppets, have someone to work the puppets to the audience, this will give you greater control of response and behaviour. That person can also place the visuals in place on the board at the relevant points. If you do not have a puppet theatre, use the puppets behind an overturned table or behind an armchair or between curtains. Have the children sit behind a certain line in a defined area and ask them not to go beyond the line.

- Have an alternative to chocolate especially for the Lids game.

Welcome time

The beginning of a session is a busy time, with everyone arriving, meeting up with friends, freeing children from the constraints of car seat or buggy, or setting out equipment, preparing refreshments and maybe taking money. But greeting the children and the adults who bring them is a time when you can really make them welcome in a special way. The ideas given on these pages aim to give you a structure for making that 'hello' an experience which affirms everyone in the group.

You could use a different welcome time idea each time you meet. Or select one which suits your group and use that to launch your time together every session. This will help build a sense of group identity so that even very young children will start to join in with a regular and repeated introduction. It will become the signal for the group to come together, to settle and to look forward to what is going to happen next.

Your group may have a fluid start time – if so, save your welcome for a time when the whole group comes together, maybe for some singing or a story, or before refreshments.

If you start at a set time, have an informal sing-song or news sharing for a few minutes before your regular welcome, so that stragglers have an opportunity to arrive and join in.

Tiddlywinks: The Big Yellow Book has ideas for welcoming everyone to your group plus extra ways of welcoming new children or visitors, saying a positive 'hello' to parents and carers, and for celebrating birthdays.

Turn to pages 94 and 95 for home time ideas.

There are more welcome time ideas in other 'Big Books' in the *Tiddlywinks* range.

1

Welcome time idea

We hope you'll stay
This getting-to-know-you game welcomes each child by name, making them feel welcome and noticed. It will help the other children to get to know one another's names and help you too! After each verse, encourage the child to share some news or make a positive comment to them.

> There's a girl called Sophie, she is here today,
> We're glad Sophie is our friend and we hope she'll stay.
> There's a boy called Robert, he is here today,
> We're glad Robert is our friend, and we hope he'll stay.

Have an individual carpet square for each child for your all-together time. Children love to choose a colour or pattern and the individual squares encourage them to sit by themselves or with their carer without climbing over their little friends or wandering about. Carpet warehouses and shops regularly throw out samples or sell them off cheaply: if you ask in advance and are prepared to pick up from the shop you may get them for free. Many shops are happy to oblige non-profit making groups for young children.

2

Welcome time idea

Who will be a friend?
This game is a variation of 'The farmer's in his den'. All stand in a circle together and choose a confident child to start the game off by standing in the middle. The game can be played several ways: 'Martin' can find a friend(s); or one or more children can leave the circle, go to Martin and bring him back with them into the ring. For the second verse, all hold hands in the circle and move around.

> Martin's all alone,
> Martin's all alone,
> Who will be his friend,
> So he's not alone?
>
> Together we can dance!
> Together we can sing!
> We praise God together,
> He gives us everything.

Welcome time idea
Say 'hello'
This idea can be adapted, depending on the number of children in the group. Begin with a verse of 'If you're happy and you know it'. Then keep the same tune as you welcome each child in turn.

> If you're happy and you know it, clap your hands,
> If you're happy and you know it, clap your hands,
> If you're happy and you know it, and you want us all to know it,
> If you're happy and you know it, clap your hands.
>
> If you're Mary and you know it, say 'hello',
> If you're Mary and you know it, say 'hello',
> If you're Mary and you know it, and you want us all to know it,
> If you're Mary and you know it, say 'hello'.

Mary says 'hello' and everyone says 'hello' back.

Repeat for all the children in the group. If the size of the group makes this unwieldy, up to four children at a time can be welcomed. Don't worry about having to 'bend' the tune a little to fit the names in!

> If you're Matthew and you know it, say 'hello',
> If you're Daisy and you know it, say 'hello',
> If you're Maniel and you know it, say 'hello' so we will know it,
> If you're Alex and you know it, say 'hello'.

Welcome time idea
Teddy on the lap
For this game you will need a teddy or similar cuddly toy and a large dice. (Make your own by stuffing a large cube-shaped packaging box with crumpled scrap paper. Seal down all flaps. Cover the box in coloured paper and draw on large black dots with a marker pen.) Begin with everyone sitting in an inward-facing circle, preferably on a carpeted area, and with the teddy sitting on an adult's lap. Ask a child (either the one sitting next to the teddy or choose at random) to roll the dice. Count the dots together. Then count that number of places round the circle and pass the teddy on to that person. Ask the children if they can guess whose lap the teddy will sit on next. Look out for children who are getting frustrated because the teddy doesn't land on their laps, and invite them to roll the dice and to give extra help with the counting.

You can play 'Teddy on the lap' at home time too.

Welcome to adults
Prepare a welcoming letter or leaflet about your group. Include practical details like where to park, where the toilets are and any fee or charge for refreshments as well as names and contact numbers of group organisers and the purpose of the group.

Mention other events that happen on the premises and other activities for pre-school children – and for adults too – in your area.

If you print this on folded card, about the size of a wallet or purse, it will be durable and easy to carry around.

Use the reverse side of the children's 'take-home' activity pages to print your own news: events coming up, invites to church services, reminders plus anecdotes and news about people in your group.

Welcome to new children or visitors
Our book
As an ongoing activity, build up a large loose-leaf scrapbook with each child having their own page. (Use thin card or stiff paper, at least A3 size. The book will be handled a lot so needs to be sturdy. Cut and reinforce holes at one edge and bind with string or ribbon.) When new children come, show them the book and explain what it is. Then show them 'their' page and write their name clearly at the top. Add the new page and a recent photograph.

Encourage the children to add to their own page, from week to week. Let them add what they choose: pictures of their family, home, themselves, toys, bus tickets, dried leaves... anything they wish. Chat to individual children about their own pages; or use the book with a few children, looking through and talking about it together.

Happy Birthday
Decorate a large cardboard box to be a 'birthday post box'. Make a slit for posting letters and a door which can be opened on one side. Before your session, put any cards or gifts for the birthday child (children) into the box.

During your circle time or when everyone is together, show the box and ask the children what it is: after a couple of uses, they will be eager to tell you. 'Discover' that today there is some post in the box and invite the appropriate child to come and get their very own post. They may like to bring an adult (parent, carer, group helper) with them. Say or sing 'happy birthday'.

Most children will want to open their post straight away but don't be surprised if some prefer to take it away for later.

You could 'check' the box every time, or only when there is post inside.

93

Home time

The end of a session can be chaotic, with some people in a rush to leave, others still chattering, children tired and fractious or still full of energy and reluctant to be strapped into a buggy or to wear a coat. Leaders may be busy clearing up and cleaning up. But a positive home time can make each person – child and adult – feel they are valued and encourage them to come another time.

You could use a different home time idea each time you meet. Or select one which suits your group and use that to close your time together every session. This will help build a sense of group identity so that even very young children will start to join in with a regular and repeated 'goodbye'. It will help each member of the group to feel part of a community – even one which only lasts an hour – and to affirm each person there.

If you finish at a set time, select a home time activity to use as the last item of your programme. Make sure you allow enough time so that people don't feel they have to hurry off or miss this part.

If your group is less structured, choose a time when you are all together, towards the end of the session.

Make home time a definite event and avoid having people putting away equipment or clearing up at the same time: aim to include and involve everyone.

Tiddlywinks: The Big Yellow Book has ideas for saying 'goodbye' to everyone in your group plus extra ways of marking 'milestone' events: those going to a new area or leaving the group to start school.

Turn back to pages 92 and 93 for Welcome time ideas.

There are more home time ideas in other 'Big Books' in the *Tiddlywinks* range.

1
Home time idea
Shout it out!
This rhyme or praise shout will give a positive ending to a worship time together or simply to end your session with a child-friendly 'benediction'.

Praise God, praise God,
Praise him with our clapping,
Praise him with our waving,
Praise God, praise God,
Praise him with all our hands.

2
Home time idea
Everyone can see
At the end of a session, it's good to think about what has been going on and how we have spent time together. Young children are developing concepts of friendship and this action rhyme gives some structure and words to express those early understandings. Choose a verse that seems most appropriate for your group or use the whole rhyme. Everyone will be able to join with actions.

If you give your smile to me,
I'll give my smile to you.
Then everyone can see
Just what a smile can do.

If you wave to me,
I will wave to you.
Then everyone can see
Just what a wave can do.

If you shake hands with me,
I'll shake hands with you.
Then everyone can see
Just what a handshake can do.

3
Home time idea
God is with us
Lead this song, with everyone echoing each phrase, to the tune of 'Frère Jacques'. You can vary the mood by making this gentle and thoughtful or noisy and bright, either from time to time, or by repeating the song words and changing the rhythm and volume.

God is with us,
God is with us,
Yes he is,
Yes he is.
He will never leave us,
And we know he loves us,
Yes he does,
Yes he does.

4
Home time idea
Let's all toot!
This is a noisy ending game with plenty of opportunity to move about and play musical instruments. Stand or sit still for the first verse, while blowing trumpets; stay still or move about as you shake rattles and maracas during the second verse; march around during the third verse, playing drums. All stand still and play vigorously for the fourth verse; then march again, past the storage box for the instruments so putting them away is part of the game! In the last verse, change 'goodbye' if another word is in common use with your children.

Let's all toot together.
Toot, toot, toot,
Toot, toot, toot.
Let's all shake together.
Shake, shake, shake,
Shake, shake, shake.
Let's all drum together.
Bang, bang, bang,
Bang, bang, bang.

Let's all play together.
(All play instruments together.)
(March and put instruments away.)
Let's thank God/Jesus for each other.
Thank you. Thank you.
Thank you. Thank you.
Let's say goodbye to each other.
Goodbye. Goodbye.
Goodbye. Goodbye.

Get Ready Go

A child's first day at school is a big moment for them... and you. But while some children can't wait to get started, others might not be so confident. Making sure your children are ready to go is really important.

Get Ready Go! is a brilliant new book for children about to start primary school. Using simple words, bright pictures and fun activities, *Get Ready Go!* explains what school is going to be like, helping your children prepare for that exciting first term.

Get Ready Go! comes complete with a companion guide for parents, packed with useful advice so that you can help them get ready too.

Get Ready Go! is a great new resource for all Early Years educators and can also be used by primary schools as a central part of their induction programme.

A colourful three-book set in an envelope, available singly or in packs of 10. Each set contains:

Get Ready to Let Go

'Have I put enough in her lunchbox?' Essential preparation for families and parents.

Get Ready Go!

'What's it going to be like?' A clear, friendly guide to help children talk and think about the big adventure of starting school!

Individual set – £2.99 ISBN 1 84427 132 0
Pack of 5 – £10.00 ISBN 1 84427 133 7

Going to school

I can do it!
Use the pictures on the inside back cover of this book to make an individual poster or scrapbook for each child who is starting school. Over several weeks, before the child leaves, play games and do activities to help them learn each of these life skills which will be useful when they go to school:

- Putting on your coat
- Taking off/putting on your own shoes
- Fastening buttons
- Working a zip fastener
- Recognising your own name, when it's written down
- Writing your name
- Using cutlery
- Managing the toilet by yourself
- Washing hands
- Blowing nose, using a paper tissue

When each skill has been learned, let them colour in the relevant picture on their own chart or book page.

Add other skills or specific tasks that your local schools like children to know, eg clipping wet weather boots together with a peg, knowing your telephone number.

Involve parents and carers in learning these skills – and make sure you keep it enjoyable and don't cause children added worry about going to school.

Moving away

From all of us
Prepare a leaving card or poster for the child or family. You could decorate it with children's own artwork, informal group photos or use a large commercially available greetings card. Let everyone in the group 'sign' it in their own way – with a drawing, a name, a scribble. Print the children's names by the side, if it is not clear who has done the writing.

Have you enjoyed this book?

Then take a look at the other Big Books in the *Tiddlywinks* range.
Why not try them all?

The Big Orange Book
Themes: What's inside God's big book? All creatures great and small; Friends of God; Stories of Jesus
978 1 85999 716 1

The Big Red Book
Themes: Christmas is coming; People we meet; Stories Jesus told; God gives us food
978 1 85999 658 4

The Big Blue Book
Themes: All about me; God gives us... homes, clothes, food, etc; People who knew Jesus; Friends of God
978 1 85999 657 7

The Big Yellow Book
Themes: Easter; God gives us families; Friends of Jesus; What's the weather like?
978 1 85999 692 8

The Big Purple Book
Themes: Jesus love me; God love it when I... make music, sing, dance, look at books, I'm 'me'; Friends and followers; Materials and technology
978 1 85999 719 2

The Big Green Book
Themes: God's wonderful world; God gives us people; Let's find out about Jesus; God knows when I'm... happy, cross, sad, scared, busy
978 1 85999 695 9

'I love this! It's great!' Sarah, leader of a 3 to 5s group in Victoria, Australia.

'...really pleased wi your material and l forward to integra Tiddlywinks into our existing programme. Marion, Scotland

Tiddlywinks Big Books are designed for use in any pre-school setting. The multi-purpose outlines are packed full of play, prayers, crafts, stories and rhymes; simply pick and mix ideas to meet the particular needs of your group. You'll find plenty of practical advice on setting up and running a pre-school group, plus ideas in every session to help you include adult carers. The children will love the illustrated activity pages.
A4, 96pp, £11.99 each

You can order these or any other *Tiddlywinks* resources from:
- Your local Christian bookstore
- Scripture Union Mail Order: Telephone 01908 856006
- Online: log on to www.scriptureunion.org.uk/shop to order securely from our online bookshop

Also now on sale
Glitter and Glue. Say and Sin Even more craft and prayer ideas for use with under fiv